NEW SCOTTISH WRITING

Edited by Harry Ritchie

BLOOMSBURY

First published 1996

This paperback edition published 1997

This anthology © 1996 by Bloomsbury Publishing PLC

Loose Continuity by William Boyd first appeared in the *New Yorker*.
Proem and *(1)* and *(2)* by Tom Leonard
first appeared in the *Lines Review*.
Mrs Quasimodo's Divorce first appeared in the *Poetry Review*.

The copyright of the individual contributions
remains with the respective authors © 1996

The moral right of the authors have been asserted

Bloomsbury Publishing PLC, 38 Soho Square, London W1V 5DF

A CIP catalogue record for this book
is available from the British Library

ISBN 0 7475 3161 7

10 9 8 7 6 5 4 3 2 1

Typeset by Hewer Text Composition Services, Edinburgh
Printed in England by Clays Ltd, St Ives plc

CONTENTS

CONTENTS

INTRODUCTION

By Harry Ritchie

As I remind myself every time I get into a drunken fight while lasciviously counting my change and adjusting my bandana of soiled lint, racial stereotypes, like all generalisations, are wrong. However, having acknowledged that, and bearing in mind Angus Calder's astute observations later in this book about the complexity of the Scottish identity as well as our reputation, I'll risk claiming that many Scots do share certain traits. One of which is a tendency, given half the chance, to go on a bit about the glories of Scotland.

I could no longer overlook this characteristic after an English acquaintance returned recently from his first trip north of the border. I was geared up for the usual eulogy – the wondrousness of the landscape, the warmth of his reception, the creaminess of the eighty-shilling. What I received instead was a diatribe because, in the three days he had spent working in Scotland, he had been constantly subjected to a litany of boasts. He now knew, for example, that Scotland's geology was the oldest in the world, that Scotland had had four universities when England only had two, that Celtic were the first British club to win the European Cup, and that Scots had invented, among other things, the steam engine, the telephone, television, the modern road surface, open-air nursery schools, political economy, whisky, golf and the rainproof coat. I think he finally cracked near Blairgowrie, where he was required to admire the planet's tallest hedge.

This introduction provides me with an unmissable opportunity to indulge in some patriotic bragging of my own, for this

2   anthology is designed to celebrate the extraordinary boom now taking place in Scottish literature. So extraordinary is this boom that I have daydreamed about compiling what really would be a high-quality, well-populated and bulky anthology of work by contemporary writers from Fife. As a result, and because this book had to be the size of a book rather than a wardrobe, the task of keeping the number of contributors down to a manageable two dozen was a grim one. So, in an effort to pre-empt too much forehead-slapping about the conspicuous absences in this compilation, I would like to point out that (a) I did try to persuade Iain Banks, James Kelman, Liz Lochhead, and Muriel Spark to provide contributions but no amount of pleas or threats could alter the fact that they felt they had no contributions to provide, and (b) such is the strength and depth of Scottish writing now that drawing a blank with those four was felt to be a bit of a shame rather than a catastrophe, and (c) any outrage over other conspicuous absentees is very probably completely justified and (d) this book, not being wardrobe-sized, does not aim to provide a definitive or comprehensive line-up.

What it does aim to do is give some indication of the richness and variety, the wit, verve and range of current Scottish literature. I suspect these qualities may not be immediately obvious to those pundits who air the impression that, when you open a new book by any Scot, out will inevitably stagger a rabidly cursing cast of the down-at-heel and down-and-out. Although it has clearly been strengthened by the Rab C Nesbitt cultural stereotype, this literary cliché owes more, I think, to selective speed-readings (at best) of the hugely and deservedly successful James Kelman and Irvine Welsh, as well as knee-jerk responses to the fact that many of the most important contemporary Scottish writers are, if not working-class, then certainly not posh.

This is something of a phenomenon. Even at the height of its dedication to proletarian literature, the Stalinist Congress of Soviet Writers could come up with little more than crazed attacks on allegedly bourgeois books, yet the most celebrated characters in recent Scottish fiction have been the likes of

Kelman's bus conductor Hines and Alan Warner's superstore skivvy Morvern Callar. Indeed, the working-class context of much contemporary Scottish literature has been so distinctive that it has distracted attention from the superb achievements of Candia McWilliam and William Boyd.

The noticeably lower-class nature of some of its most prominent subject-matter, language and authorial CVs has also encouraged claims that the wonderful upsurge in Scottish writing has somehow been propelled by the political Zeitgeist. Put crudely – and to be honest they never really merit a nicer adverb – these claims state that Scotland found new energy in its literature – and in its art, popular and classical music, media, comedy (in fact, just about every aspect of its culture bar, sadly, its football) – in reaction to the political traumas of 1979, when the devolution bid failed shamefully and Thatcher patronised her way into power.

The explanation is attractive, right enough, because it fosters the image of a culture being created by people who have manned the barricades of disenfranchised self-expression, shaking a fist at the bastards in Whitehall who compensated for closing down our industries by making Malcolm Rifkind Foreign Secretary. Unfortunately, the trouble with that sort of grand cultural overview is that it lacks anything that vaguely resembles research or evidence.

To avoid any waffle, I am tempted to ascribe Scotland's literary boom to the forces of pure, blind coincidence, but perhaps a more persuasive explanation is that one literary achievement encourages another. Poetry has been flourishing here ever since the Scottish Renaissance led by Hugh MacDiarmid in the 1920s. The vigour in fiction is much more recent, beginning in 1981 when Alasdair Gray unleashed his first book, *Lanark*, and thereby proved just how daft had been the speculations that there was something in our psyche or culture or diet that had rendered Scots inherently incapable of writing great novels. A couple of years later, when the Polygon Press published his first major books, James Kelman showed just

4   what could be done by writing in a resolutely vernacular voice. Other inspirational examples have been provided by the likes of the ever-innovative Edwin Morgan, the quietly skilful Iain Crichton Smith, the wonderful Douglas Dunn, and, of course, the late and much-lamented Norman MacCaig.

To tell the truth though, like everyone else I don't really know why or how Scottish writing has so many great talents, from those older authors with their tremendous bibliographies to those such as A.L. Kennedy and Duncan McLean, who have already achieved excellence and who can have only the haziest memories of the first Moon landing. In the end, I'd rather not try to explain but stick to the boasting, which I can indulge in with great justification. As this anthology shows.

SHREDDING THE ICEBERGS

By Candia McWilliam

The hot days when the wasps came and trudged all over the scallops with their legs and feelers and the Fantas sold faster than the teas at the seafood stall; on such days I used to see these *types* congregating and I would ask myself where will the human race end? Looks like a contest between in the gutter singing glory and so neat you'd need to wear a headsquare to procreate.

I would think: where did these different kinds of souls get born and how do they hatch? Do they take one another in as they dither about, or do they walk right the way through each other like ghosts? It was my job to hand out the sustenance to these tribes, so that meant I was implicated, just like a keeper in the zoo handing over the bucket of sprats or peelings. It was my doing these folk got the energy to stand up, stick around, walk about the town, pull out their wallets in exchange for a few more items to lose, and struggle on to the boats without fainting from hunger on account of not having had a snack between after lunch coffee and early afternoon tea, or between that one last drink and the first of the evening.

These hot days were when the body paid for carrying on as if your skin could be forever hidden under wool. In this context, Scottish people come off particularly poorly. Unpeeled, we have a selection of looks, unless there's been a genetic accident and the body's holding up against the punishment. We're spare and sandy, or red and beety, or sweaty and soft with burning cheeks and meeting eyebrows, or blue-skinned blondes with the junkie posture who go old overnight at twenty-eight or the second baby. The men are redhaired or blackhaired and mostly wronghaired,

6 sprouting at the shoulder blade or tailend or inner arm. I'm not complaining though. Duncan is a freak of nature and the kids take after him. They've all got his sweatless skin and black eyes, his white teeth and tidy form. They look like kids in a film made for childless adults. I look like a mother. What people have aye said about me is, 'It's a mercy she's nice eyes. Her eyes are nice.'

They're nothing like me at all, to look at, the kids. The wonder is that he took me and the answer is the usual one. He was tired of the success and the freedom. He never understood why he had been given them, did not know how to use them, and was relieved when they weren't there any more and I was there instead, keeping them off, success, freedom and the women, all the three.

We run the stall together and Joanne and Ian and Dougie help in the school holidays. Joanne's gone veg so she does not do cockles or whelks but she is neater at garnish than the boys and she washes up the crocks with the water out the tea urn faster than any of us.

In the cold, we keep a brazier outside the stall, and we've a plastic tent with stripes like a seaside one, where we get a bit of shelter from the wind. We tried selling the snacks right indoors, but it slumped. There was no spirit of adventure for the customers eating prawns in Marie Rose sauce off a clamshell in a shelter.

It's more of a sport, more of a holiday, to do it outside in the biting wind or salty rain. And on the hot days, though there are fewer of those, they swarm around the stall, but they won't go inside for fish, only drinks and ices, and even then they prefer to walk around with those. When they've finished, they leave their tins and cartons and implements right there, with less thought than a dog shitting. It's as if the wrappers and cans and wee wooden forks are as natural as leaves.

I'd go round, or Duncan would, with a big bin lined with a black liner, like someone collecting pennies after a Punch and Judy show. They'd all look baffled and turn to their friends or family in order to avoid our eyes. I never approached them till they were finished the tub of mussels or the ocean stix, and you'd think they'd welcome a place to put the rubbish, but they seem to need it to talk with, like a beast marking a place before feeling at home.

Occasionally you'd get one who was considerate. They'd pick a piece of debris off the ground, carry it carefully to the bin, drop it in with a little twitch of distaste, repeat the operation and then keep this up with ever smaller specks of rubbish till you looked up and thanked them, which was what they wanted, because then they could explain to you how much better it would be if you packed the whole operation up in cabbage leaves, or offered a fully automated rubbish chuting device such as they know a man who makes fine examples of not far out of town, it's a starter enterprise on a wee grant from the Board and he's heard we're not doing so bad how about a partnership with his friend, o.k. he won't be modest, it's the man himself standing right here on this spot my word but those shrimps were good and that pink sauce was unusual.

On the hot days the smells from the kitchens of the steamers that go out to the islands hang around this pier and the gulls don't bother to move off further than three feet away from the stall. Then we cut the lettuce into ribbons round the back and I sort it into clamshells ready for the fish when the orders come. We don't reckon to sell the sample dishes we put out the front under cling, so they're what the gulls get. In the sun the shellfish turns. It goes a grey pink and smells of primary school pants.

The sunset comes so late sometimes I'm counting shellfish into lettuce at eleven at night. The wasps are gone by then, but the cats come and lie right on your feet, buzzing with the assumption that all fish is theirs by law. Ian and Dougie shoogle them off their trainers, but Joanne and her dad slip them soused herring over the sell-by and the remains of milk crushes. In the stall it smells of vinegar and commercial strawberry and smoked fish. If there's shredded lettuce over, I bag it up and put it in the fridge for tomorrow, and any fish that won't stretch another

8 day, I take it over to the bench on the esplanade where there's always someone been slowed down on their evening struggle home from the hotels. I can usually offer them a roll or two as well. They sit there shouting out intimate comments to the closed-up face of Woolworths and the Royal Bank, standing up to attack the night from time to time till it beats them down to sleep.

We start at five in the morning, even after a hot day. In summer it's blue and you can hear the day beginning on the islands close-in, the doors opening, the outboards coming to life. Later the tractors start up, bringing the children down to the jetty to come over to school here on the mainland. The fishing boats are coming in after the night, their men making coffee. I watch the boats come in off the edge of the sea. There are mornings the water's flat and silver over beyond Lismore and the boats seem to tug the skyline in with them as they come, tight behind each boat in a V., till it's pulled so thin it melts away when the boat's alongside. I used to watch Duncan fretting these mornings and I'd fetch his tea and quiz him about it, is it sweet enough, would he be wanting more and so on.

This annoyed him but it kept him off the thoughts he'd been having. His brothers Tam and Gordon go out on the boats. They've part ownership of the *Hera*, out of Islay, and they make a living that can be good depending on the catch. They've a deal over the clams and crabs with a man runs a restaurant for rich tourists up at Port Appin. They would pour scorn on Duncan's and my booth and our prices to fit the pocket. Their wives shop in Glasgow for their clothes. Tam has a woman as well down by Dunstaffnage he'd buy the coats for and take out for meals while Moira bides in and gets her pound of flesh in the form of a car. At family occasions, their kids wouldn't mix with ours. They'd ask them the odd question so's it'd look normal, but the questions would be phrased like geography questions to remote tribespeople. It's like they'd never met kids before that didn't have the things they had. They couldn't rightly see people that weren't dressed the way they thought was right.

Duncan's and my kids carried on the rivalry, if you could call it that with only the one side competing, by looking like their father. Their cousins are all decked out in their loose, grubby-coloured gear with the words on it and the slobbering trainers with the tongues out, but the spots and tufts and bulges aren't away just because your shirt says Quicksilver Surfwear and cost three lobster dinners and a half of Smirnoff. And they scratch. They scratch in under these clothes and pull out from their body's crevices small finds they sook out from their nails with a sleepy look, or rind off on bits of paper, or ball up and flick without looking where they're going.

I anticipated no change but heaviness, no new life, in these young cousins of my children. These are the ones, I would think, will live as they do till they burst from heart or get shrunk by the cancer. It's a tussle which thing they take's going to get them first. Suffocation from the cigs, gagging from the takeouts, blootering into extinction from the drink, or the shove out into the morgue from one small pill or a final poison smoke. At least with our kids, I'd say to Duncan, there's the option of a climbing accident. Don't mind me, I just used to say these things.

The kids swore the other things are out of the question, though I would never be sure they'd played safe till I could see them certified pure on the autopsy table aged seventy-five, like all mothers of my sort, the anxious kind, the ones can't believe their luck.

In the snow, that comes more rarely to us here beside the sea than intheways a few miles and up by the Ben, the snacks we sell go in the deep frier Duncan and I bought for our twelfth anniversary from the mail order. It's a lid goes on over the squiggling fish pieces inside, you scoop it all out with a slotted spoon, dish it out on greaseproof and shake over the vinegar. Hand it out fast as you can fry it up and the hot smell moves along the pier with the wind.

Strangers talk to one another eating hot food in the snow. They don't eating the cold snacks in the heat. It's to do with my

10 theory that folk don't enjoy things that come too comfortable. Standing in the snow, with the white islands on one side and the raw hill on the other, the sea actually under their feet that slip about on the pier, these people behave as though they've made their way over twenty miles of ice to make it to our wee booth, even though there's the hotels over the way, the railway cafeteria and the Chinese up the alley behind Chalmers and MacTavish's selling the twenty different carryout potato fillings.

The best day in snow we've had at the booth was this January, right after the New Year. It was that chilly I'd invested in the gloves with the cut-off fingertips and a wee flap goes over like a mitten, so you've got the movement of the fingers and the recovery period for them after inside the top bit that goes over like an egg cosy.

There was one of these groups of folk around that isn't any shape, just humans not seeing each other, the tall ones with guncases letting dogs in and out of cars, the other ones not wearing enough clothes and shouting at one another from close up and telling jokes without listening. There was some call for the soup I keep on the go, it was kidney bean and lamb skirt, Duncan was busy at the frier, and Joanne was cutting monk tail for the mixed seafood medley. The boys were preparing the two coatings in the back, batter and breadcumbs. It offers a choice to the mouth. Men take crumb and the women batter, I find. But I can be wrong. After all, it's a crude division, sorting people into sexes.

Then up the pier comes a wee thing on high bootee heels, with an umbrella covered with yellow flowers. Her feet leave treads small as marks in pastry in the snow. She's giggling like a bird. The seagull next to her looks as if it could pick her up by its beak with the one orange dot on its hook. She's Japanese, come to see this other wee country that's made such a success out of the whisky.

Her man is reversing down the pier away from her but towards us, his black loafer shoes going blacker with the snow, and the turn-ups in his trousers collecting it. He's snapping her

of course, and she's posing with a soft handful of snow, her face
up squint to it like a bunch of flowers, breathing in the crystals,
and blowing them off the snow in her hands out to him and to
us. It's the kind of snow takes its time about landing. It twirls
and rests in any light it can get.

We're watching her as she leaves these little steps as small as
the gulls' triangular plods, but pointing the other way, the way
she's coming. The light is the snowlight of glary grey though
the mountain is all white, and the islands are blue and yellow in
the folds of their whiteness. The brazier is black and blue and red
and the frier fills the air with a bottled-up hissing. I notice that
the characters around our family booth have become a group.
They have been woken up for a while from themselves.

Down the pier she comes with her snow posy and we watch
her yellow-flowered umbrella come closer behind her, her bit
of private weather.

Just as the Japanese man's about to catch his raincoat on the
brazier, two men budge and pick it up to move it, taking care
to adjust it between the relative heights of their grips, so the
coals on the top stay level. Nothing disturbs the glow of the
brazier. The heat between the coals is like red mortar. Only
the ash shifts and falls, leaving a grey trail in the snow.

The Japanese man turns round, perhaps feeling the heat
moving back and away from him in the cold Western air,
and seems to be taking it all in, the plastic striped tent, the
fried food in paper, the redfaced people of differing largeness,
the brown dog with a tuna-coloured nose, the black one whose
tail has drawn a fan in the snow, and he includes us all in his
greeting, 'Good evening.'

By the time the girl has arrived and shaken the snow off her
woolly gloves, he is half way round the individuals who now
compose a group around the brazier outside the tent where I
hoped to keep my family safe from the world outside. I flip
back the knitted snoods of my mitts, and begin to use my
fingers, until I am almost enjoying the sensations they are prey
to, bitter cold, a stinging where the vinegar gets into the cuts

12 I'm never without, the chill glittery ribbons of iceberg, the hot stubbled shell of the fritters made with crumb, the light deflatable sheen of the battered fish. I enjoy the dexterity the exposure has given me.

Ian and Dougie and Joanne are posing for the camera in the snow outside our small striped plastic tent. The couple take several more snapshots of the group. More snacks are ordered. I thin the soup to make it go round, it's so thick after its day reducing in the stockpot.

In Japan, someone will almost certainly think that the booth is where we live, up here among the snows and floating islands of the West Coast. They will see our brazier and the people around it and in their minds will arise some idea of the tribes within which we live, huddled together for warmth, waiting for boats to take us away to islands in warmer waters, accompanied by dogs and protected by taller men with guns.

You can take it any way you need to.

Since round about then, I've been letting the children out and about that bit more. Duncan has gone shares with a man sets creels not far out beyond Kerrera. We'll sell the lobster here from the tent on the pier, when we get some.

The year is outwith my control, as it always was. I am letting the days come in with what they carry and leave with what we can give them. When I cut the icebergs into these light shreds, the thing that was the size of a head is spun out and the gaps between its smithereens filled in with a thousand layers of air so you get a basin of stuff airier than lawnmowings and sparkling like fibreglass. And so the days go on, chopped into finer and finer shreds of lightness that I think at last I can feel, each one, just before it goes.

THE TIME OF MY LIFE

By Michael Cannon

'Cameron!'

    'Sir?'

    'What were the terms of the Secret Treaty of Dover!'

    Expectant silence from my cronies.

    'I can't tell you, sir. It's a secret.'

    If any kid had said that off the cuff to me I'd have given them marks for initiative. Not him. His judicious nod as he fetched the belt from the drawer. 'Belt' is a total misfuckingnomer. 'Belt' can suggest something designed to prevent one's trousers from falling down and regaling a classroom of small boys with the sight of one's arse, or worse, pants that one's mum bought for one, suitable for casual wear or impromptu parachutes. Wrong. 'Belt' can even suggest a huge great big bloody thing used to encompass vast trunks full of the paraphernalia of Victorian families, preventing these containers from bursting open on railway platforms in a huge deluge of stays and elaborate feminine lingerie. Wrong again. It's not just that I fondly nurture a penchant for women's underwear – a predilection to which I freely admit and which occasioned many a surreptitious and murky foray into my mother's Freeman's Catalogue – 'Belt' to me connotes a huge great big fucking thing made of black boiled leather and called things by the manufacturer guaranteed to strike terror in the stoutest schoolboy heart, which mine wasn't. Names like 'Lochgelly Double X'. 'Belt' is a thing that uncoiled like a snake and, when wielded by the adroit, cut the air like a steam whistle to land with singular effect on the hands of obstreperous small Scottish schoolboys.

14   There are many types of pause: the rude pause, on the telephone ignoring the gesticulations of a colleague; the pregnant pause, favourite of the literati; the sensuous pause, as with the lips of lovers hovering a hair's breadth from one another in tremulous anticipation. Then there is the sadistic pause. He was a master of this. He had a genius for extorting, to the nth degree, the mental anguish experienced by the victim in that awful hiatus between pronouncement of sentence and its execution. The sense of camaraderie with one's schoolfellows soon evaporates as one gets dragged out to the front and laid into with gusto. Having been a source of amusement, one becomes an object of curiosity, and indeed, macabre entertainment, as they think en masse: 'He's going to get it now, right enough. Thank fuck it's not me.' But that is human frailty and must be legislated for if not approved of.

'What hand do you write with, Cameron?'

'Write, sir?' There was no rising intonation to indicate that this was a question. If I was going to get the belt I wanted it on my good hand, to provide me with an excuse for not doing any homework.

'Spell the hand you write with.'

No luck.

I quote the incident only to prove a point. I made the joke knowing its repercussions. The prospect of notoriety, of being acclaimed class 'wag', outweighed in attractiveness the fear of pain. At least it did till the laughter subsided and I stood alone – yet another Oliver. Innate bravado, call it what you will. There are worse personae.

One year of metalwork had not sufficed to make a coat hook. With parents' night approaching, and him not wanting the blame for our sloth rubbing off, he ran around manufacturing the things small boys had botched weekly for the last three terms. In one fluid movement he snatched from me the aluminium strip I'd been abusing for months, drilled and countersank the screw holes, and, with several unerring blows dealt from a pigskin mallet, bent the piece to its prescribed curvature. It made a nonsense of my endeavours and relegated me, even in my own eyes, to a bungling pubescent.

'Bastard.'

'What?' The voice cracked with incredulity. 'What did you say, boy?'

'Bastard. I said "Bastard". This file, sir. It's a bastard.'

'Six of the best or ten of the radiator?'

Well, I mean to say. For fuck's sake. Taking one look at him I should have known. A blacksmith or some such thing before he persuaded himself he had a vocation. A tradesman with tradesman's hands. His hands – that's what I remember. Priam said Achilles had 'man-killing' hands. I looked at his with the same horrible fascination. These seemed impervious to heat. A grown man and a thirteen-year-old boy – not much of a competition. Better the devil you know than the devil you don't; but then, he had broad shoulders and I didn't fancy being hit by him with a bloody great belt either.

'I'll take the radiator.'

'Sir!'

'I'll take the radiator, sir.'

Oil-fired central heating. I'm padding at it tentatively when he clamps his big hand on top of mine.

'One,' he says, and then about three seconds later 'Two.'

Evidently I lasted till five, then blanched and burst into tears.

'It's the heat,' I explained to them in the playground afterwards, 'does something to the tear ducts.'

The point was, I could probably have had his arse kicked on the grounds of professional delinquency, or whatever it's called. But I felt the need to make light of it. It's the way I've always coped, or avoided coping. It was like that with women too.

I am waiting for Linda, the Stradivarius of sex. The nonpareil. My trousers have a knife-like crease, my barathea blazer recently removed from tissue paper. Linda is beautiful, my Dulcinea. Double Trigonometry is where our eyes first met, chalk dust in the sunbeams and a petulant toss of her head. The instant

16   was charged, such moments comprise life, and like Faust I bade the moment stay. I carry flowers in my hand that advertise my purpose. I am a man with a mission, careless of the scrutiny as I stand at the crossroads. My preparations have been elaborate: half a carton of talcum powder down the briefest of briefs. Why? I do not know. Were any sudden call to be made for the tackle to come into operation I would run a mile in fright. My pubic hair resembles the coiffure of a Regency rake. My crotch is a flour-mill. Such precautions are the vestige of religious guilt and the belief that clean underpants must be worn in the likelihood of an accident. They are the sine qua non of being admitted to casualty. I thought I could be denied admission to hospital, haemorrhaging torrentially on the pretext of wearing yesterday's Y-fronts. Like a sentry I stride, my path marked by puffs of dust percolating from the bottom of my trousers. I wait three hours then decide to stand her up.

'Did you do it?'

'Did I do it.' My tone is ironic. I eat my midget gems with savoir-faire. 'Did I do it.' Now shading to adult superciliousness.

'Yes – did you do it?'

'Stephen says his big sister was down the amusement arcade with Linda last night.'

'He didn't do it.'

Desultorily they drift away.

I am waiting for Deborah, the Stradivarius of sex. The nonpareil. I have a Saturday job near her. She is Aphrodite rising from the mezzanine. My preparations have been elaborate. I have gambled on the hyperbolic claims of the cologne, surreptitiously bought for the purpose. Extracts from animals' armpits swamp the smell of my own. The half pint of Wild Muskweed, or whatever it's called, which I poured over myself, announces my intention. Pedestrians savour me at thirty yards. I am a man with a mission. I radiate pheromones. My sexual signals waft the length of the Glasgow conurbation. The flowers are for Deborah, my Dulcinea. Two hours I wait and walk off convinced I have confused our rendezvous. At some other vantage point, I imagine, she will be standing, similarly bereft, a Pre-Raphaelite heroine poignantly forlorn.

'Did you do it or what?'

I decided to be frank.

'Not right away.'

'When?'

This required a masterfully worded evasion which compromised neither my masculine integrity nor her virtue.

'Afterwards.'

'After what?'

'We've decided to wait.'

'She didn't show,' someone said. 'I passed him and she didn't show.'

They snort and turn.

'What's that smell?'

I am the obvious culprit.

'You bought that stuff! He bought that stuff and she didn't show!'

I am undaunted. I am waiting for Cindy, the Stradivarius of sex. The nonpareil. Beautiful as the Shulamite in the Song of Songs. Her hair is like a flock of goats, her eyes as the pools in Heshbon. Her teeth are like a flock of ewes that are newly shorn. Her lips are like a thread of scarlet, dropping honey. Honey and milk are under her tongue. Her neck is like a tower of ivory. The joints of her thighs are like jewels, the work of the hands of a cunning workman. Her navel is like a round goblet, wherein no mingled wine is wanting. She is beautiful as Tirzah, comely as Jerusalem. The smell of her garments is like the smell of Lebanon. Her stature is like to a palm tree and her breasts to clusters of grapes.

And she didn't fucking turn up either.

I'd become a landmark by this time. I reflected on this as I booted the bouquet into the skip. 'Sharp right at the extinct volcano, hang a left at the virgin and flowers.' The virgin and flowers: sounds like a fucking English pub. Girls I'd never met

18   were queuing up to chuck me. I thought there was something genetically wrong with me. Perhaps I had a random leave-me-standing-in-the-pouring-rain-for-three-hours gene. Or a rogue join-the-gang-and-make-a-fucking-idiot-out-of-me-in-public chromosome. At any rate, I thought, who gives a toss. But even as I said it to myself I knew that I did.

I wasn't waiting for Myra who wasn't the Stradivarius of sex. Nor the nonpareil either. She never stood me up and I can't ever remember any sudden transitional point dividing when we weren't going out with one another from when we were. If our coming together was deliberate on her part it wasn't on mine. I think she found and kept me by a process of pleasant insinuation. Why? God alone knows. What she saw worthwhile in me I'll never guess. But I'm glad she did. I was still running around with bunches of dead flowers and a painful awareness of my own virginity, pursuing sexual mirages with the common sense of a dog. Next minute, holidays, love, sex (in that order, she saw to that. I was all for sex, and then more sex, and then ever more sex after that, and then having a go at the rest) and an interim of years that didn't last as long as that cow Linda tossing her head in the chalkdust. She ran to fat, I'm glad to say. 'I made wax dolls of them all,' I explained to Myra, 'and I'm working on an incantation for thrush.' She even stopped me swearing – no mean feat. Whenever I lapse now it's usually indicative of something.

These are just some of the examples I told him. I could have chosen a dozen others. They all demonstrated the same devil-may-care attitude. The bravado. I was trying to make things easy for him, fill up the silence.

'That just about brings things up to date,' I said.

The phone rang, the timing like a piece of supernatural stage managing. The acoustics were unsympathetic in that ceramic cell. He was only gone for a few minutes. I looked around at the instruments in their glass standing-case, the stainless steel kidney-shaped bowl, the bleached porcelain. He came back carrying a large brown envelope which he laid face down. I didn't say anything. I sat and waited for him to get to the sticking-place. He looked me straight in the eye, I'll always remember that, before he spoke.

'Positive.'

Well, I mean to say. For fuck's sake. No wonder they pay these people so much. I wouldn't have looked me in the eye and said 'Positive' if they'd thrown in a Ferrari and three hot-blooded mulatto concubines as part of the deal. He said there was time to discuss details later. 'All the time in the world,' I said. What details? I thanked him and took my leave. All the way home I toyed in my mind with that one little word, its inflections and repercussions.

Pos-itive. Pos-**it**-ive. Po-**sit**-ive. Posit-**ive**.

I also wandered up a few mental cul-de-sacs thinking about the laws of probability and omnibenevolence. And even the probability of omnibenevolence. Then I turned over in my mind my little stock of quotations relevant to the topic, the type of things I'd trot out in a conversation to try and give the impression I knew what the fuck I was talking about – flies and wanton boys and ripeness being all, and that type of thing. I prided myself that my conclusion was a fair summation of all these mental gymnastics, profound yet enjoying the advantage of a certain lapidary significance:

Why the fuck me?

When I got to the house I made a pot of tea which I left untasted. This is a thing I never do. 'Fucking ominous if you ask me,' I thought. And then I said aloud, 'Be positive!' It's a little pact I have with myself never to renege on a resolution I make aloud. I only make them when alone. Positive. The irony wasn't intentional and I giggled as I realised, stuffing my fingers into my mouth like an embarrassed schoolgirl. 'Pull yourself together!' I shouted.

I spent some time walking into various rooms. I found myself sitting in the one room neither of us likes. When, with increasingly profound silence, the children continued not to arrive, it wound up being a repository for all the things we

20 wouldn't throw out or find cupboard space for. We never come here – the nursery that never was. And then I thought: 'This room's like this because Myra's tests never showed positive, and now I'm here because mine did.' Just goes to show you. What the fuck it goes to show you I'll never know. People never know what half the things they say mean. And they're the clever ones. Take an expression like 'Could be worse.' There's another. 'My dog's got no nose,' I say. 'Could be worse' you answer, which, as well as being a vacuous expression, ruins a perfectly good joke. But there you go.

I seemed to discover myself sitting on an upturned tea-chest at the sound of the front door closing. She was home. I looked around at the balled-up newspaper and the clutter. Ten years and we hadn't even unpacked. In the corner lurked my dumb-bells bought in a fit of pride and enthusiasm that lasted till I had to carry them home. I could start again. It would have to be a crash course. My mortal coil could be in the peak of physical condition as it shuffled off.

I heard her walk from room to room, searching, and then climb the stair. Somehow I couldn't bring myself to shout out. Since I was in the most unlikely room, she looked in here last. My back was to the door and I couldn't bring myself to turn round either. She came and stood just behind me. I could sense her. I knew she was folding her arms, and the agitation of her face. It was obvious neither of us was paid as much as he was. I looked up, at the only room exempt from our renovations. It really was ugly.

'It's me or that wallpaper,' I said, pointing, 'one of us will have to go.'

MRS QUASIMODO'S DIVORCE

By Carol Ann Duffy

I'd loved them fervently since childhood.
Their generous bronze throats
gargling, then chanting slowly, calming me—
the village runt, name-called, stunted, lame, hare-lipped;
but bearing up, despite it all, sweet-tempered, good
  at needlework;
an ugly cliché in a field,
pressing dock-leaves to her fat, stung calves
and listening to the five cool bells of evensong.
I believed that they could even make it rain.

The city suited me; my lumpy shadow
lurching on its jagged alley walls;
my small eyes black
as rained-on cobblestones.
I frightened cats.
I lived alone up seven flights,
boiled potatoes on a ring
and fried a single silver fish;
then stared across the grey lead roofs
as dusk's blue rubber rubbed them out,
and then the bells began.

I climbed the belltower steps,
out of breath and sweating anxiously, puce-faced,
and found the campanologists beneath their ropes.
They made a space for me,

22   telling their names,
and when it came to him
I felt a thump of confidence,
a recognition like a struck match in my head,
and caught a sex smell coming from him,
coming my way.
It was Christmas-time.
The tusk that snagged his upper lip was wet with spit.
When the others left,
he fucked me underneath the gaping, stricken bells
until I wept.

We wed.
He swung an epithalamium for me,
embossed it on the fragrant air.
Long, sexy chimes,
exuberant peals,
slow scales trailing up and down the smaller bells,
an angelus.
We had no honeymoon,
but spent the week in bed.
And did I kiss
each part of him—
that horseshoe mouth,
that tetrahedron nose,
that squint left-eye,
that right eye with its pirate wart,
the salty leather of that pigs-hide throat,
and give his cock
a private name—
or not?

So more fool me.

We lived in the Cathedral grounds.
The bellringer.

The hunchback's wife.
The Quasimodos. Have you met them? Gross.
And got a life;
our neighbours – sullen gargoyles, fallen angels,
   cowled saints
who raised their marble hands in greeting
as I passed along the gravel paths,
my husband's supper on a tray beneath a cloth.
But once,
one evening in the Ladychapel on my own,
throughout his ringing of the seventh hour,
I kissed the cold lips of a King next to his Queen.
Don't ask me why.
Something had changed,
or never even been.
Soon enough,
he started to find fault.
Why did I this?
How could I that?
Look at myself.
And in that summer's dregs,
I'd see him
watch the pin-up gypsy with her goat
dancing for the tourists in the square;
then turn his discontented, traitor's eye on me
with no more love than stone.

I should have known.
Because it's better, isn't it, to be well-formed.
Better to be slim, be slight,
your slender neck quoted between two thumbs;
and beautiful, with creamy skin,
and tumbling auburn hair,
those devastating eyes;
and have each lovely foot
held in a gentle hand

24   and kissed;
then be watched till morning as you sleep,
so perfect, vulnerable and young
you hurt his blood.

And given sanctuary.

But not betrayed.
Not driven to an ecstasy of loathing of yourself;
banging your ugly head against a wall,
gaping in the mirror at your heavy dugs,
your thighs of lard,
your mottled upper arms;
thumping your belly—
look at it—
your wobbling gut.
You pig. You stupid cow. You fucking dog.
Abortion. Cripple. Spastic. Mongol. Ape.

Where did it end?
A ladder. Heavy tools. A steady hand.
And me, alone all night up there,
bent on revenge.
He had pet-names for them.
Marie.
The belfry trembled when she spoke for him.
I climbed inside her with my claw-hammer, my pliers,
   my saw, my clamp;
and, though it took an agonizing hour,
ripped out her brazen tongue
and let it fall.
Then Josephine,
his second-favourite bell,
kept open her astonished golden lips
and let me in.
The bells. The bells.

I made them mute.
No more arpeggios, or scales, no stretti, trills
for christenings, weddings, great occasions, happy days.
No more practising
for bellringers on smudgy autumn nights.
No clarity of sound, divine, articulate,
to purify the air
and bow the heads of drinkers in the city bars.
No single
solemn
funeral note
to answer
grief.

I sawed and pulled and hacked.
I wanted silence back.

Get this—

when I was done,
and bloody to the wrist,
I squatted down among the murdered music of the bells
and pissed.

LOOSE CONTINUITY

By William Boyd

I am standing on the corner of Westwood and Wilshire, just down from the Mobilgas station, waiting. There is a coolish breeze just managing to blow from somewhere, and I am glad of it. Nine o'clock in the morning and it's going to be another hot one, for sure. For the third or fourth time I needlessly go over and inspect the concrete foundation, note again that the powerlines have been properly installed and the extra bolts I have requested are duly there. Where is everybody? I look at my watch, light another cigarette and begin to grow vaguely worried: have I picked the wrong day? Has my accent confused Mr Koenig (he is always asking me to repeat myself)? . . .

A bright curtain – blues and ochres – boils and billows from an apartment window across the street. It sets a forgotten corner of my mind working – who had drapes like that, once? Who owned a skirt that was similar, or perhaps a tie?—

A claxon honks down Wilshire and I look up to see Spencer driving the crane, pulling slowly across two lanes of traffic and coming to a halt at the kerb.

He swings himself down from the cab and takes off his cap. His hair is getting longer, losing that army crop.

'Sorry I'm late, Miss Velk, the depot was, you know, crazy, impossible.'

'Doesn't matter, it's not here anyway.'

'Yeah, right.' Spencer moves over and crouches down at the concrete plinth, checking the powerline connection, touching and jiggling the bolts and their brackets. He goes round the back of the crane and sets out the wooden "Men at Work" signs, then reaches into his pocket and hands me a crumpled sheet of flimsy.

'The permit,' he explains. 'We got 'til noon.'

'Even on a Sunday?'

'Even on a Sunday. Even in Los Angeles.' He shrugs. 'Even in 1945. Don't worry, Miss Velk. We got plenty of time.'

I turn away, a little exasperated. 'As long as it gets here,' I say with futile determination, as if I had the power to threaten. The drape streams out of the window suddenly, like a banner, and catches the sun. Then I remember: like the wall hanging Utta had done. The one that Tobias bought.

Spencer asks me if he should go phone the factory but I say give them an extra half hour. I am remembering another Sunday morning, sunny like this one, but not as hot, and half the world away, and I can see myself walking up Grillparzer Strasse, taking the shortcut from the station, my suitcase heavy in my hand, and hoping, wondering, now that I have managed to catch the early train from Sorau, if Tobias will be able to find some time to see me alone that afternoon . . .

Gudrun Velk walked slowly up Grillparzer street, enjoying the sun, her body canted over to counterbalance the weight of her suitcase. She was wearing . . . (What was I wearing?) She was wearing baggy cotton trousers with the elasticated cuffs at the ankles, a skyblue blouse and the embroidered felt jacket with the motif of jousters and strutting chargers. Her fair hair was down and she wore no make-up; she was thinking about Tobias, and whether they might see each other that day, and whether they might make love. Thinking about Utta, if she would be up by now. Thinking about the two thick skeins of still-damp blue wool in her suitcase, wool that she had dyed herself late the night before at the mill in Sorau and that she felt sure would finish her rug perfectly, and, most importantly, in a manner that would please Paul.

Paul looked in on the weaving workshop often. Small, with dull olive skin and large eyes below a high forehead, eyes

28 seemingly brimming with unshed tears. He quietly moved from loom to loom and the weavers would slip out of their seats to let him have an unobstructed view. Gudrun had started her big knotted rug, she remembered, and he stood in front of it for some minutes, silently contemplating the first squares and circles. She waited: sometimes he looked, said nothing and moved on. Now, though, he said: 'I like the shapes but the yellow is wrong, it needs more lemon, especially set beside that peach colour.' He shrugged, adding, 'In my opinion.' That was when she bought his book and started to go to his classes on colour theory – and she had unpicked the work she had done and began again. She told him: 'I'm weaving my rug based on your chromatic principles.' He was pleased, she thought. He said politely that in that case he would follow its progress with particular interest.

He was not happy at the Institute, she knew; since Meyer took over, the mood had changed, was turning against Paul and the other painters. Meyer was against them, she had been told, they smacked of Weimar, the bad old days. Tobias was the same: 'Bogus-advertising-theatricalism,' he would state, 'we should've left all that behind'. What the painters did was 'decorative', need one say more? So Paul was gratified to find someone who responded to his theories instead of mocking them, and in any case the mood in the weaving workshops was different, what with all the young women. There was a joke in the Institute that the women revered him, called him 'the dear Lord.' He did enjoy the time he spent there, he told Gudrun later, of all the workshops it was the weavers he would miss most, he said, if the day came for him to leave – all the girls, all the bright young women.

Spencer leans against the pole that holds the powerlines. The sleeve of his check shirt falls back to reveal more of his burned arm. It looks pink and new and oddly, finely ridged, like bark or like the skin you get on cooling hot milk. He taps a rhythm on the creosoted pole with his thumb and the two remaining fingers on his left hand. I know the burn goes the length of his arm and then some more, but the hand has taken the full brunt.

He turns and sees me staring.

'How's the arm?' I say.

'I've got another graft next week. We're getting there, slow but sure.'

'What about this heat? Does it make it worse?'

'It doesn't help, but . . . I'd rather be here than Okinawa,' he says. 'Damn right.'

'Of course,' I say, 'of course.'

'Yeah.' He exhales and seems on the point of saying something – he is talking more about the war, these days – when his eye is caught. He straightens.

'Uh-oh,' he says. 'Looks like Mr Koenig is here.'

Utta Benrath had dark orange hair, strongly hennaed, which, with her green eyes, made her look foreign to Gudrun, but excitingly so. As if she were a half-breed of some impossible sort – Irish and Malay, Swedish and Peruvian. She was small and wiry and used her hands expressively when she spoke, fists unclenching slowly like a flower opening, thrusting, palming movements, her fingers always flexing. Her voice was deep and she had a throaty, man's chuckle, like a hint of wicked fun. Gudrun met her when she had answered the advertisement Utta had placed on the noticeboard in the students' canteen: 'Room to rent, share facilities and expenses.'

When Gudrun began her affair with Tobias, she realised she had to move out of the hostel she was staying in. The room in Utta's apartment was cheap and not just because the apartment was small and had no bathroom: it was inconvenient as well. Utta, it turned out, lived a brisk forty-five-minute walk from the Institute. The apartment was on the top floor of a tenement block on Grenz Weg, out in Jonitz with a distant view of a turgid loop of the Mulde from the kitchen window. It was clean and simply furnished. On the walls hung brightly coloured designs for stained glass windows that Utta had drawn in Weimar.

30 Here in Dessau she was an assistant in the mural-painting workshop. She was older than Gudrun, in her early thirties, Gudrun guessed, but her unusual colouring made her age seem almost an irrelevance: she looked so unlike anyone Gudrun had seen before that age seemed to have little or nothing to do with the impression she made.

There were two bedrooms in the apartment on Grenz Weg, a small kitchen with a stove and a surprisingly generous hall where they would eat their meals around a square scrubbed pine table. They washed in the kitchen, standing on a towel in front of the sink. They carried their chamber pots down four flights of stairs and emptied them in the night soil cistern at the rear of the small yard behind the apartment building. Gudrun developed a strong affection for their four rooms: her bedroom was the first of her own outside of her parents' house; the flat was the first proper home of her adult life. Most evenings, she and Utta prepared their meal – sausage, nine times out of ten, with potatoes or turnip – and then, if they were not going out, they would sit on the bed in Utta's room and listen to music on her phonograph. Utta would read or write – she was studying architecture by correspondence course – and they would talk. Utta's concentration, Gudrun soon noticed, her need for further qualifications, her ambitions, were motivated by a pessimism about her position in the Institute to which all talk inevitably returned. She was convinced that the mural-painting workshop was to be closed and she would have to leave. She adduced evidence, clues, hints that she was sure proved that this was the authorities' intention. Look what had happened to stained glass, she said, to the wood and stone carving workshops. The struggle it had taken to transfer had almost finished her off. That's why she wanted to be an architect: everything had to be practical these days, manufactured. Productivity was the new God. But it took so long, and if they closed the mural-painting workshop . . . Nothing Gudrun said could reassure her. All her energies were devoted to finding a way to stay on.

'I've heard that Marianne Brandt hates Meyer,' she reported

one night, with excitement, almost glee. 'No, I mean really hates him. She detests him. She's going to resign, I know it.'

'Maybe Meyer will go first,' Gudrun said. 'He's so unpopular. It can't be nice for him.'

Utta laughed. And laughed again. 'Sweet Gudrun,' she said and reached out and patted her foot. 'Never change.'

'But why should it affect you?' Gudrun asked. 'Marianne runs the metal workshop.'

'Exactly,' Utta said, with a small smile. 'Don't you see? That means there'll be a vacancy, won't there?'

Mr Koenig steps out of his car and wrinkles his eyes at the sun. Mrs Koenig waits patiently until he comes round and opens the door for her. Everyone shakes hands.

'Bet you're glad you're not in Okinawa, eh, Spence?' Mr Koenig says.

'Fire from heaven, I hear,' Spencer says with some emotion.

'Oh, yeah? Sure sounds that way.' Mr Koenig turns to me. 'How're we doing, Miss Velk?'

'Running a bit late,' I say. 'Maybe in one hour, if you come back?'

He looks at his watch, then at his wife. 'What do you say to some breakfast, Mrs Koenig?'

Tobias liked to be naked. He liked to move around his house doing ordinary things, naked. Once, when his wife was away, he had cooked Gudrun a meal and asked her to eat it with him, naked. They had thick slices of smoked ham, she remembered, with a pungent radish sauce. They sat in his dining room and ate and chatted as if all was perfectly normal. Gudrun realised that it sexually aroused him, that it was a prelude to love-making, but she began to feel cold and before he served the salad she asked if she could go and put on her sweater.

Tobias Henzi was one of the three Masters of Form who ran the architecture workshop. He was a big burly man who

32   would run seriously to fat in a few years, Gudrun realised. His body was covered with a pelt of fine dark hair, almost like an animal, it grew thickly on his chest and belly and, curiously, in the small of his back, but his whole body – his buttocks, his shoulders – was covered with this fine glossy fur. At first she thought she would find it repugnant, but it was soft, not wiry, and now when they were in bed she often discovered herself absentmindedly stroking him, as if he were a great cat or a bear, as if he were a rug she could pull round her.

They met at the New Year party in 1928 where the theme was 'white'. Tobias had gone as a grotesque, padded pierrot, a white cone on his head, his face a mask of white pancake. Gudrun had been a colonialist, in a man's white suit with a white shirt and tie and her hair up under a solar topee. By the party's end, well into January 1st, she had gone into an upstairs lavatory to untie her tight bun, vaguely hoping that loosening her hair would ease her headache.

Her hair was longer then, falling to her shoulders, and as she came down the stairs to the main hall she saw, sitting on a landing, Tobias – a large, rumpled, clearly drunken pierrot, smoking a dark knobbled cigar. He watched her descend, a little amazed, it seemed, blinking as if to clear some obstruction to his vision.

She stepped over his leg, she knew who he was.

'Hey, you,' he shouted after her. 'I didn't know you were a woman.' His tone was affronted, aggressive, almost as if she had deliberately misled him. She did not look round.

The day the new term began he came to the weaving workshop to find her.

I take my last cigarette from the pack and light it. I sit on the step below the cab of Spencer's crane, where there's some shade. I see Spencer coming briskly along the sidewalk from the pay phone. He's a stocky man, with the stocky man's vigorous rolling stride, as if the air is crowding him and he's shouldering it away, forcing his passage through.

'They say it left an hour ago.' He shrugged. 'Must be some problem on the highway.'

'Wonderful.' I blow smoke into the sky, loudly, to show my exasperation.

'Can I bum one of those off of you?'

I show him the empty pack.

'Lucky Strike.' He shrugs, 'I don't like them, anyway.'

'I like the name. That's why I smoke them.'

He looks at me. 'Yeah, where do they get the names for those packs? Who makes them up? I ask you.'

'Camel.'

'Yeah,' he says. 'Why a camel? Do camels smoke? Why not a . . . a hippo? I ask you.'

I laugh. 'A pack of Hippos, please.'

He grins and cuffs the headlamp nacelle. He makes a *tsssss* sound, and shakes his head, incredulously. He looks back at me.

'Goddam factory. Must be something on the highway.'

'Can I buy you some breakfast, Spencer?'

Paul met Tobias only once in Gudrun's company. It was during one afternoon at four o'clock when the workshops closed. The weavers worked four hours in the morning, two in the afternoon. The workshop was empty. The big rug was half done, pinned up on an easel in the middle of the room. Paul stood in front of it, the fingers of his right hand slowly stroking his chin, looking, thinking. From time to time he would cover his left eye with his left palm.

'I like it, Gudrun,' he said, finally. 'I like its warmth and clarity. The colour penetration, the orangey-pinks, the lemons . . . What's going to happen in the bottom?'

'I think I am going to shade into green and blue.'

'What's that black?'

'I'm going to have some bars, some vertical, one horizontal, with the cold colours.'

He nodded and stepped back. Gudrun, who had been standing

34 behind him, moved to one side to allow him a longer view. As she turned, she saw Tobias had come into the room and was watching them. Tobias sauntered over and greeted Paul coolly and with formality.

'I came to admire the rug,' Paul said. 'It's splendid, no?'

Tobias glanced at it. 'Very decorative,' he said. 'You should be designing wallpaper, Miss Velk, not wasting your time with this.' He turned to Paul. 'Don't you agree?'

'Ah. Popular necessities before elitist luxuries,' Paul said, wagging a warning finger at her, briefly. The sarcasm sounded most strange coming from him, Gudrun thought.

'It's a way of putting it,' Tobias said. 'Indeed.'

We sit in a window of a coffee shop in Westwood Village. I've ordered a coffee and Danish but Spencer has decided to go for something more substantial: a rib-eye steak with fried egg.

'I hope the Koenigs don't come back,' Spencer says. 'Maybe I shouldn't have ordered the steak.'

I press my cheek against the warm glass of the window. I can just see the back end of Spencer's crane.

'I'll spot them,' I say. 'And I'll see the truck from the factory. You eat up.'

Spencer runs his finger along the curved aluminium beading that finishes the table edge.

'I want you to know, Miss Velk, how grateful I am for the work you've put my way.' He looks me in the eye. 'More than grateful.'

'No, it is I who am grateful to you.' I smiled. 'It's not easy to find someone more reliable.'

'Well, I appreciate what you—'

His steak comes and puts an end to what I'm sure would have been long protestations of mutual gratitude. It's too hot to eat pastry so I push my Danish aside and wonder where I can buy some more cigarettes. Spencer, holding his fork like a dagger in his injured left hand, stabs it into his steak to keep it steady on the plate, and, with the knife in his right, sets about trying to saw the meat into pieces. He is having difficulty: his thumb and two fingers can't keep a good grip on the fork handle, and he saws awkwardly with the knife.

'Damn thing is I'm left-handed,' he says, sensing me watching. He works off a small corner, pops it in his mouth and then sets about the whole pinioning, slicing operation again. The plate slides across the shiny table top and collides with my coffee mug. A small splash flips out.

'Sorry,' he says.

'Could I do that for you?' I say. 'Would it bother you?'

He says nothing and I reach out and gently take the knife and fork from him. I cut the steak into cubes and hand back the knife and fork.

'Thank you, Miss Velk.'

'Please call me Gudrun,' I say.

'Thank you, Gudrun.'

'Gudrun! Gudrun, over here.' Utta was beckoning from the doorway of Tobias's kitchen. Gudrun moved with difficulty through the crowd, finding a gap here, skirting round an expansive gesture there. Utta drew her into the kitchen, where there was still quite a mob, too, and refilled Gudrun's glass with punch and then her own. They clinked glasses.

'I give you Marianne Brandt,' Utta said, quietly. She smiled.

'What do you mean?'

'She did resign.'

'How do you know? Who told you?'

Utta discreetly inclined her head towards the window. 'Irene,' she said. Standing by the sink talking to three young men was Irene Henzi, Tobias's wife. Gudrun had not seen her there. She had arrived at the party late, uneasy at the thought of being in Tobias's house with his wife and other guests. Tobias had assured her that Irene knew nothing, Irene was ignorance personified, he said, the quintessence of ignorance. Utta carried on talking – some business of amalgamation, of metal, joinery

36 and mural-painting all being coordinated into a new workshop of interior design – while Gudrun covertly scrutinised her hostess. Irene did not look to her like an ignorant woman, she thought, she looked like a woman brimfull of knowledge. '– I told you it would happen. Arndt's going to run it. But Marianne's refused to continue . . .' Utta was saying but Gudrun did not listen further. Irene Henzi was tall and thin, she had a sharp long face with hooded, sleepy eyes and wore a loose black gown that seemed oddly Eastern in design. To Gudrun she appeared almost ugly and yet she seemed to have gathered within her a languid, self-confident calm and serenity. The students laughed at something she said, and with a flick of her wrist which made them laugh again, she left them, picking up a plate of canapés and beginning to offer them to the other guests standing and chatting in the kitchen. She drifted towards Utta and Gudrun, closer, a smile and a word for everyone.

'I have to go,' Gudrun said, and left.

Utta caught up with her in the hall where she was putting on her coat.

'What's happening? Where are you going?'

'Home. I don't feel well.'

'But I want you to talk to Tobias, find out more. They need a new assistant now. If Tobias could mention my name, Meyer would listen to him . . .'

Gudrun felt a genuine nausea and simultaneously, inexplicably, infuriatingly, an urge to cry.

Spencer frowns worriedly at me. I look at my watch, Mr Koenig looks at his watch also and simultaneously the truck from the factory in Oxnard rumbles up Wilshire. Apologies are offered, the delays on the highway blamed – who would have thought there could be so much traffic on a Sunday? – and Spencer manoeuvres the crane into position.

Tobias ran his fingertips down her back to the cleft in her buttocks. 'So smooth,' he said, wonderingly. He turned her over and nuzzled her breasts, taking her hand and pulling it down to his groin.

'Utta will be home soon,' she said.

Tobias groaned. He heaved himself up on his elbows and looked down at her. 'I can't stand this,' he said. 'You have to get a place of your own. And not so damn far away.'

'Oh yes, of course,' Gudrun said. 'I'll get a little apartment on Kavalierstrasse. So convenient and so reasonable.'

'I'm going to miss you,' he said. 'What am I going to do? Dear Christ.'

Gudrun had told him about the dyeing course she was going to take at Sorau. They met regularly now, almost as a matter of routine, three, sometimes four times a week in the afternoon at the apartment on Grenz Weg. The weaving workshop closed earlier than the other departments in the Institute and between half past four and half past six in the afternoons they had the place to themselves. Utta would obligingly stop for a coffee or shop on her way home – dawdling for the sake of love, as she described it – and usually Tobias was gone by the time she returned. On the occasions they met he seemed quite indifferent, quite unperturbed at being seen.

'Now, if Utta was the new head of the metal workshop,' Gudrun said, 'I'm sure she'd be much more busy than—'

'– don't start that again,' Tobias said. 'I've spoken to Meyer. Arndt has his own candidates. You know she has a fair chance. A more than fair chance.' He put his arms around her and squeezed her strongly to him. 'Gudrun, my Gudrun,' he exclaimed, as if mystified by this emotion within him. 'Why do I want you so? Why?'

They heard the rattle of Utta's key in the lock, her steps as she crossed the hall into the kitchen.

When Tobias left, Utta came immediately to Gudrun's room. She was dressing, but the bed was still a mess of rumpled sheets, which for some reason made Gudrun embarrassed. To her the room seemed to reek of Tobias. She pulled the blanket up to the pillow.

38 'Did he see you when he left?' Gudrun asked.

'No, I was in my room. Did he say anything?'

'The same as usual. No, "a more than fair chance", he said. But he said Arndt has his own candidates.'

'Of course, but a "more than fair chance". That's something. Yes . . .'

'Utta, I can't do anything more. I think I should stop asking. Why don't you see Meyer yourself?'

'No, no. It's not the way it works here, you don't understand. It never has. You have to play it differently. And you must never give up. Never.'

Spencer checks that the canvas webbing is properly secured under the base, jumps down from the truck and climbs up to the small control platform beside the crane.

I explain to Mr Koenig: 'It's manufactured in three parts. The whole thing can be assembled amazingly quickly. It's painted, finished. We connect the power supply and you're in business.'

Mr Koenig was visibly moved. 'It's incredible,' he said. 'Just like that.'

I turn to Spencer and give him a thumbs up. There's a thin puff of bluey-grey smoke and the crane's motor chugs into life.

Tobias sat on the edge of his desk, one leg swinging. He reached out to take Gudrun's hand and gently pulled her into the V of his thighs. He kissed her neck and inhaled, smelling her skin, her hair, as if he were trying to draw her essence deep into his lungs.

'I want us to go away for a weekend,' he said. 'Let's go to Berlin.'

She kissed him. 'I can't afford it.'

'I'll pay,' he said. 'I'll think of something, some crucial meeting.'

She felt his hands on her buttocks; his thighs gently clamped hers. Through the wall of his office she could hear male voices from one of the drafting rooms. She pushed herself away from him and strolled over to the angled drawing table that was set before the window.

'A weekend in Berlin . . .' she said. 'I like the sound of that, I must—'

She turned as the door opened and Irene Henzi walked in.

'Tobias, we're late,' she said, glancing at Gudrun with a faint smile.

Tobias sat on, one leg swinging slightly.

'You know Miss Velk, don't you?'

'I don't think so. How are you?'

Somehow Gudrun managed to extend her arm; she felt the slight pressure of dry cool fingers.

'A pleasure.'

'She was at the party,' Tobias said. 'Surely you met.'

'Darling, there were a hundred people at the party.'

'I won't disturb you any further,' Gudrun said, moving to the door. 'Very good to meet you.'

'Oh, Miss Velk.' Tobias's call stopped her, she turned carefully to see Irene bent over the drawing table scrutinising the blueprint there. 'Don't forget our appointment. 4.30 again?' He smiled at her, glanced over to make sure his wife was not observing and blew her a kiss.

At the edge of a wood of silver birches behind the Institute was a small meadow where, in summer, the students would go and sunbathe. And at the meadow's edge a stream ran, thick with willows and alders. The pastoral mood was regularly dispelled, however – and Gudrun wondered if this was why it was so popular with the students – by the roaring noise of aero engines. The tri-motors which were tested at the Junkers Flugplatz, just beyond the pine trees to the west, would bank round and fly low over the meadow as they made their landing approaches. In the summer the pilots would wave to the sunbathing students below.

Gudrun walked down the path through the birch wood, still

40   trembling, still hot from the memory of Tobias's audacity, his huge composure. She was surprised to see Paul coming up from the meadow. He was carrying a pair of binoculars in his hand. He saw her and waved.

'I like to look at the aeroplanes,' he said. 'In the war I used to work at an aerodrome, you know, painting camouflage. Wonderful machines.'

She had a flask of coffee with her and spontaneously offered to share it with him. She needed some company, she felt, some genial distraction. They found a place by the stream and she poured coffee into the tin cup that doubled as the flask's top. She had some bread and two hard-boiled eggs which she ate as Paul drank the coffee. Then he filled his pipe and smoked, while she told him about the dyeing course at Sorau. He said he thought she needed a more intense blue to finish her rug, something hard and metallic, and suggested she might be able to concoct the right colour at the dyeworks.

'With Tobias,' he said suddenly, to her surprise, 'when you're with Tobias, are you happy?'

He waved aside her denials and queries. Everyone knew about it, he told her, such a thing could not be done discreetly in a place like the Institute. She need not answer if she did not want to, but he was curious. Yes, she said, she was very happy with Tobias. They were both happy. She said boldly that she thought she was in love with him. Paul listened. He told her that Tobias was a powerful figure in the architecture school, that all power in the Institute emanated finally from the architecture workshop. He would not be surprised, he said, if one day Tobias ended up running the whole place.

He rose to his feet, tapped out his pipe on the trunk of a willow and they wandered back through the birch wood.

'I just wanted you to be aware about this,' he said, 'about Tobias.' He smiled at her. 'He's an intriguing man.' His features were small beneath his wide pale brow, as if crushed and squashed slightly by its weight. There were bags under his eyes, she noticed; he looked tired.

'You're like a meteor,' he said. 'Suddenly you're attracted by the earth and are drawn into its atmosphere. At this moment you become a shooting star, incandescent and beautiful. There are two options available: to be tied to the earth's atmosphere and plummet, or to escape, moving back out into space' – she was baffled at first, but then remembered he was quoting from his own book, something she had heard in his class – 'where you slowly cool down and eventually extinguish. The point is you need not plummet,' he said, carefully. 'There are different laws in different atmospheres, freer movements, freer dynamics. It need not be rigid.'

'Loose continuity,' she said. 'I remember.'

'Precisely,' he said, with a smile. 'There's a choice. Rigid continuity or loose.' He tapped her arm lightly. 'Do you know, I think I may be interested in buying your rug.'

Spencer tightens the final bolt and crosses the street to join us on the opposite sidewalk. Mr Koenig, Mrs Koenig, Spencer and me. It is almost midday, and the sun is almost insupportably bright. I put on my sunglasses and through their green glass I stare at the Koenig's mini-diner.

Mr Koenig turns away and takes a few paces, his finger held under his nose as if he is about to sneeze. He comes back to us.

'I love it, Miss Velk,' he says after apologising for the few private moments he has needed. 'I just . . . It's so . . . The way you've done those jutting-out bits. My God, it even looks like a sandwich – the roll, the meat . . . so clever, so new. How it curves like that, that style—'

'– Streamline moderne, we call it.'

'May I?'

He puts his hands on my shoulders and leans forward and up (I am a little taller) and he gives me a swift kiss on the cheek.

'I don't normally kiss architects—'

I try not to smile as I contemplate my personal refutation of everything the Institute stood for. 'Oh, I'm not an architect,' I say. 'I'm just a designer. It was a challenge.'

Gudrun never really knew what happened as the stories changed so often in the telling, and there were lies and half lies all the time. The truth made both guilty parties more guilty and they thought to absolve themselves by pleading spontaneity, and helpless instinct, but they had no time to compare notes and the discrepancies hinted at quite another version of reality.

Gudrun climbed the last block from the station and quietly opened the door of the apartment on Grenz Weg. It must have been a little before eight o'clock in the morning. She took a few steps into the hall when she heard a sound in the kitchen. She pushed open the door and Tobias stood there, naked, with two cups of steaming coffee in his hands.

His look of awful incomprehension changing to awful comprehension lasted no more than a second. He smiled, set down the cups said, 'Gudrun –' and was interrupted by Utta's call from her bedroom. 'Tobias, where's that coffee, for heaven's sake?'

Gudrun picked up a coffee cup and walked into Utta's room. She wanted Utta to see, there was to be no evasion of responsibility. Utta was sitting up in her bed, pillows plumped behind her, the sheet to her waist. Tobias's clothes were piled untidily on a wooden chair. She made a kind of sick, choking noise when Gudrun came in. For a moment Gudrun thought of throwing the hot coffee at her, but at that stage she knew there were only seconds before she herself was going to break, so, after a moment of standing there to make Utta see, to make her know, she dropped the cup on the floor and left the apartment.

Two days later Tobias asked Gudrun to marry him. He said he had gone to the apartment on Saturday night (his wife was away) thinking that was the day Gudrun was returning from Sorau. Why would he think that? she asked, they had talked about a Sunday reunion so many times. Once in his stream of protestations he had inadvertently referred to a note – 'I mean, what would you think? a note like that' – and then, when questioned – 'What note? Who sent you a note?' – said he was becoming confused – no, there was no note, he had meant to say she *should* have sent him a note from Sorau, not relied on him to remember, how could he remember everything, for God's sweet sake?

Utta. Utta had written to him, Gudrun surmised, perhaps in her name, the better to lure him: 'Darling Tobias, I'm coming home a day early, meet me at the apartment on Saturday night. Your own Gudrun . . .' It would work easily. Utta there, surprised to see him. Come in, sit down, now you're here, come all this way. Something to drink, some wine, some schnapps, maybe? And Tobias's vanity, Tobias's opportunity, and Tobias's weakness, would do the rest. Now, darling Tobias, this question of Marianne Brandt's resignation . . .

In weary moments, though, other possibilities presented themselves to her. Older duplicities, histories and motives she could never have known about and wouldn't want to contemplate. Her own theory was easier to live with.

Utta wrote her a letter: '. . . no idea how it happened . . . some madness that can infect us all . . . an act of no meaning, of momentary release.' Gudrun was sad to lose Utta as a friend, but not so sad to turn down Tobias's proposal of marriage.

I say goodbye to Spencer as he sits in the cab of his crane looking down at me. 'See you tomorrow, Gudrun,' he says with a smile, to my vague surprise, until I remember I had asked him to call me Gudrun. He drives away and I rejoin Mr Koenig.

'I got one question,' he says. 'I mean, I love the lettering, don't get me wrong – "sandwiches, salads, hot dogs" – but why no capital letters?'

'Well,' I say, without thinking, 'why write with capitals when we don't speak with capitals?'

Mr Koenig frowns. 'What? . . . yeah, it's a fair point. Never thought of it that way . . . Yeah.'

My mind begins to wander again, as Mr Koenig starts to

44   put a proposition to me. Who said that about typography? Was it Albers? Paul? ... No, Moholy Nagy, László in his red overalls with his lumpy boxer's face and his intellectual's spectacles. He is in Chicago, now. We've all gone, I think to myself, all scattered.

Mr Koenig is telling me that there are fifteen Koenig mini-diners in the Los Angeles area and he would like, he hopes, he wonders if it would be possible for me to redesign them – all of them – in this streamlined, modern streamline sort of style.

All scattered. Freer. Freer movements, freer dynamics. I remember, and smile to myself. I had never imagined a future designing hot-dog stands in a city on the west coast of America. It is a kind of continuity, I suppose. We need not plummet. Paul would approve of me and what I have done, I think, as a vindication of his principle.

I hear myself accepting Mr Koenig's offer and allow him to kiss me on the cheek once more – but my mind is off once again, a continent and an ocean away in drab and misty Dessau. Gudrun Velk is trudging up the gentle slope of Grillparzer Strasse, her suitcase heavy in her hand, taking the shortcut from the station, heading back to the small apartment on Grenz Weg which she shares with her friend Utta Benrath and hoping, wondering, now that she has managed to catch an early train from Sorau, if Tobias would have some time to see her alone that afternoon.

KATE CLANCHY

Hometime

When my grandfather died he saw,
he said, not death's bare head, but aunts,
his antique aunts in crackling black,
come to call him back from play.

Of Course

I'd tell you everything: how
daffodils are shoving shoots
through last year's leaves
heaped up, gone soft, how

a friend of mine has got
a growth that's stopping her,
which I think of as furred,
like mould, but which

has made her bald and brave
as the walnut-head Far Eastern nun
who begged me on the train
to shove her off at Hammersmith

where she drifted like a leaf
among metal-gray commuters

46   calling *Bush, Shepherd's Bush*
    as if it meant everything. I'd talk

as if you knew the way of things,
could tell me, if you chose,
the patterns of stoppage,
the reasons for growth, as if

you'd be, my love, of any use.

The Personals

The one with herpes sounded best—
who didn't mention solvency
his *soh*, his arts degree
nor say he'd *ltm*
a younger lady, petite, slim
ns, South-East, for arts pursuits—
but talked of this secret sore of his,
this soiling, suppurative lust.

Letter

You'd be surprised how we've all got on
and by the brash new block athwart your room—
four raw floors of yellow brick – and how
we've grown around your gap by now
the way the vine outside the house
twines blindly round and round itself
and the tendrils thrust their twisted shapes
over the railing into empty space.

It hit Jane worst, she keeps your voice
on an ansaphone tape inside a box,
thinks of you at least once a day,
expects us all to suddenly die.

I knew you hardly half as well,
but think of you in the swimming pool.
I brought you once, you lost your key
lit up outside, and that reminds me—

Jane met three men. One appalled me
frankly. And, Sally, pretty wilful Sally
well, she got God, went Anglo-Catholic
then to Santiago and came back pregnant.

ACT 2

If you aged like that, as shown on stage—
came home to find the same set changed,
new chairs, strange walls you didn't choose,
and the heads turned towards you were doused
in powder, as if the ceiling had fallen
in a shower of plaster and they'd sat on,
too stupid, too surprised, to unarch their brows
or flex their faces, crack the latex rows
of jowls, scrape at thick wrinkles applied
with a pencil, wipe the dust from rheumy eyes—

would you laugh, do you think, or walk
back through the paper door and run amok
behind the scenes, locate the lout
in charge of lights, the wiseass guy who wrote
the script, demand the truth, the truth, or ram
a fist through those crisp unlikely walls?
Or would you, as you've done in practice,
cross to mother played by an older actress
hear calmly, as you stooped to kiss her,
your own voice, older, speak your lines?

A FAULT ON THE LINE

By Irvine Welsh

As far as it went wi me it wis aw her ain fuckin fault. The cunts at the hoaspital basically agreed wi ays n aw, no that they said as much in so many words, bit ah could tell they did inside. Ye ken how it is wi they cunts, they cannae jist come oot and say what's oan thir fuckin mind like that. Professional fuckin ettiquitte or whatever the fuck they call it. Well seein as ah'm no a fuckin Doaktir then, eh! Ah'd last aboot five fuckin minutes wi they cunts, me. Ah'll gie yis fuckin bedside manner, ya cunts.

Bit it wis her ain fault because she kent that ah wanted tae stey in fir the fitba this Sunday; they hud the Hibs-Herts game live oan STV. She goes, – Lit's take the bairns doon tae that pub it Kingsknowe, the one ye kin sit ootside ay.

– Cannae, eh, ah sais tae ur, – fitba's oan it three. Hibs fuckin Herts.

– Wi dinnae huv tae stey long Malky, she sais, – it's a rerr day. It wid be good fir the bairns.

So ah thinks tae masel, mibee no too bad an idea but. Ah mean, ah hud ma bevvy in the fridge fir the game, bit a few scoops beforehand would set ays up nicely fir the kickoaf. So ah sais, – Aye, awright then, but wir no steyin oot long mind, the fitba's oan at three so wi huv tae be back by then. So ah'm thinkin, lit hur git hur ain wey n it'll keep her fuckin trap shut for a bit.

So wi gits oot, n it wis a rare day n aw. Wi heads along tae the fuckin pub n wi starts gittin a few peeves sunk back: her oan the voddy n hooches n me oan the pints ay Carlsberg. The bairns ur happy enough wi thir juice n crisps, even though ah hud tae batter him for pillin her hair whin the cheeky wee cunt thought ah wisnae lookin. Eh goat a shock awright whin ah gave um a fuckin wrap acroass the jaw. Ah sais, – Aye, n dinnae fuckin well burst oot greetin like a wee lassie Jason, or yill fuckin well git another yin!

Anywey, ah've goat an eye oan the fuckin cloak, fir the fitba likes, but she's flingin thum back like fuck n whin ah says it wis time tae drink up n move, she starts. – Kin we no jist stey fir one mair, she's gaun, n ah'm gaun, – Awright, bit jist a fuckin quick yin mind, then wi fuckin well Johnny Cash.

So ah fling back ma pint but she's fuckin well strugglin. That's her aw ower: thinks she kin fuckin well take a peeve, but she cannae handle it when it comes tae the fuckin bigtime. Ah jist tells her, – C'moan. We need tae fuckin nash. So ah nod tae the bairns n thair comin doon the road wi me, n she's laggin behind, the fuckin fat cow thit she is. That wis the main reason that it wis her fault; too fuckin well fat, the doaktir said it; he fuckin well telt the cunt, fuck knows how many times, eh. Ah'm shoutin, – C'moan!

Course, aw she kin dae is tae gie ays that fuckin look which gits ma fuckin goat.

– Git movin, n dinnae well pit that fuckin face oan, ah telt the cunt.

So wi gits intae Kingsknowe Station n ah goes, wi kin cut through here. She turns roond n starts walkin doon the platform tae that overheid bridge. Ah goes, – C'moan tae fuck ya radge, n jumps straight doon oantae the tracks, ken. She starts makin a fuckin exhibition ay hersel: gaun oan aboot the train comin, n ah should be able tae see that cause ay the people at the platform. – Aye, bit you're forgettin something, ah goes, ah used tae work for the railways. This wis before me n wee Tam Devlin goat the boot. The bevvy, ken? The cunts git as stroppy as fuck aboot that. Even a couple ay pints, that's you fuckin well snookered. N ah wisnae the fuckin worse, bit it wis scapegoatin, as the cunt fae the union pit it. No thit that did much fuckin good but, eh no.

– Bit it's comin! she sais, thir aw waitin oan it! Ah deeks at the fuckin cloak at the station n goes, – it's no due fir another five minutes yit! Moan tae fuck! Ah takes wee Claire n lifts her doon oantae the track, n we go ower n ah lift her up ontae the platform at the other side. The laddie, that wee cunt Jason, he's ower like a shot n she finally waddles oaf the fuckin platform doon oantae the track. Fuckin embarrassment that fat cunt.

So ah've goat the bairns up oantae the platform, then ah hears this tinny noise and the track under ma feet starts tae vibrate. It sounds like one ay they intercity non-stoapin joabs. Ah jist fuckin tipples: these cunts've been diverted tae here cause ay that flood damage oan the other line. Ah minded readin aboot that shite in the *News*. So ah'm up sharpish and ah'm sayin tae this fat cunt: – Gie's yir fuckin hand!

Well, ah grabs her mit, but the fuckin speed oan this inter-city joab; ah mean these cunts seem like thir gaunny rip the whole fuckin station apart the speed they go through it at, an wi her bein that fuckin hefty, well, ah managed tae sort ay half git her up oantae the platform and she's screamin aboot the bairns and ah'm sayin the fuckin bairns ur awright, fuckin move, but the fuckin train comes along and it fuckin well hits her, n ah jist feels this force, pillin her, wrenchin her right ootay ma fuckin grip.

Well ah fuckin well jist aboot shat masel, ah'm fuckin well tellin yis. Whin ah looks up ah'm half expectin her tae be in fuckin Aberdeen or somewhere like that, ken, bit she's only a few feet away fae ays further doon the platform n she's lookin up at ays n shoutin: – You, ya fuckin stupit cunt, at me, in front ay every cunt in the station, eh. So ah'm tellin her tae shut her fuckin mooth or she'll git ma fuckin boot in it and tae git up oaf her fat erse n git a fuckin bend oan n wee Claire's laughin n ah looks at Jason and he's jist standin thaire frozen tae the fuckin spot, eh, so ah'm aboot tae lamp the wee cunt whin ah look doon at her n ah realise that she's goat nae fuckin legs; it's like the fuckin train hud jist clean whipped thum oaf, n she's tryin tae come taewards ays crawlin along the fuckin platform, pillin hersel wi her hands and thirs this trail ay blood comin fae her.

The radgest thing aboot it aw is that ah looks doon the platform n ah sees the fuckin legs, jist sort ay severed fae her boady. At the thigh likes, eh, the baith ay thum. So ah shouts at the wee cunt: – Jason! Dinnae jist fuckin stand thair, pick up yir Ma's legs! Git a hud ay thum! Ah wis thinkin thit ye could git thum tae the hoaspital n git thum stitched back oan. The wee bastard jist starts greetin, right oot ay fuckin control. Some cunt's shoutin tae git an ambulance, n she's lyin on the groond cursin n ah'm thinkin aboot the fuckin fitba, kick oaf in ten fuckin minutes time. But then ah gits tae thinkin thit the ambulance'll maist likely huv tae go past oor bit oan its wey up tae the hoaspital n ah could bail oot n catch up wi her back up thair, eftir the game likes. So ah starts gaun, – Too right mate. A fuckin ambulance then, eh.

Wee Claire's went ower tae her Ma's legs n she's picked thum up, gathered thum in her airms and she's running taewards ays, n ah lits that sneaky wee cunt Jason huv it, right acroas the fuckin jaw n eh fuckin well felt that yin cause that stoaps ehs greetin right away. – You fuckin well should've goat they legs ya daft wee cunt, fuckin leavin it up tae yir wee sister! She's only a bairn! How auld ur ye? Eight! Fuckin well act it!

This auld cunt's doon at her side hudin her hand and sayin, – Yir awright, it'll be fine, the ambulance is on its wey, try tae be still, n aw that shite. Another guy says tae me, – My god, this is terrible. Ah jist goes, – Fuckin well surein it is, probably missed the first two goals, eh. This nondy cunt comes up tae ays n sais, – I know you must be under terrible stress but it'll be okay. She's hanging in there. Try to comfort the children. Ah jist goes, – Aye, right ye are.

So ah sais tae the bairns, jist as the ambulance comes, – Yir Ma's gaun tae the hoaspital fir a bit, but thir's nowt wrong wi her.

– She's loast her legs, wee Claire goes.

– Aye, ah ken that, but thir's nowt wrong wi her, no really. Ah mean, aye, fir anybody else, anybody ordinary likesay you

52   or me, it wid be bad tae huv nae legs. But no fir yir Ma ·cause she's that fat she widnae be able tae git roond oan her legs that much longer anywey, ken?

    – Will Ma die? Jason asks.

    – Ah dinnae ken. Ah'm no a fuckin Doaktir, um ah? Dinnae ask such daft questions Jason. What a laddie for fuckin questions. See if she does, n ah'm no sayin thit she will, but see if she does, jist sayin, right? Jist supposin thit she wis tae die, n this is jist sayin mind . . .

    – Like pretend, wee Claire goes. Mair brains thin her fuckin Ma, that yin.

    – That's right hen, jist pretend. So if she wis tae die, n mind, wir only sayin *wis*, it's up tae youse tae be good n no tae gie me a hard time, cause ye ken what ah'm like when ah start gittin a hard time. Ah'm no sayin thit ah'm wrong n ah'm no sayin thit ah'm right; aw ah'm sayin is dinnae youse be giein ays a hard time at a time like this. Or yis git this, right? ah goes, clenchin ma mit n shakin it at the wee cunts.

    So by the time the ambulance boys manage tae lug her intae the fuckin van, wi her fuckin weight, the game'll huv already sterted. Ah takes the legs oaf the bairn n goes tae lob them in the back wi her, but this ambulance boy takes them n wraps them in polythene n ice. We gets in n the back wi her n the boy thit's drivin's waistin nae time. Whin wir near our bit n ah sais, – Ah'll jist bail oot it the roundabout ahead mate.

    – Eh, the boy goes.

    – Jist lit ays oaf here, ah sais.

    – Wir no stoapin here mate, we're no stoapin until we git tae the hoaspital. Nae time tae lose. You'll need tae register your wife and look after the kids here.

    – Aye right, ah goes, but ah wis still thinkin ahead, – Is thir a telly oan the wards mate? Bound tae be bit, eh.

    This cunt jist looks at ays aw funny like n then goes, – Aye, thirs a telly.

    A fuckin wide cunt. Anywey, she's goat that oxygen mask ower her face n the guy's gaun oan tae her aboot tae try no tae talk n ah'm thinkin: some fuckin chance, ah've been tryin tae git her no tae talk fir fuckin years, eh. Hearin her n aw: gaun oan tae me like it's ma fuckin fault. It wis her wantin mair fuckin drink as usual, pished up cow. Ah telt her, if ye spent as much time lookin eftir the fuckin bairns as ye did oan the fuckin pish, then they might no be so far behind at the school, especially that wee cunt Jason. Ah turns tae him n goes, − Aye, n dinnae think thit you're jist gaunny doss oaf the school, jist because yir fuckin Ma might be in dock fir a few weeks. You'd better fuckin well shape up son, ah'm tellin ye.

Sometimes ah think tae masel that ah'm giein the wee cunt too much ay a hard time. Bit then ah go: naw, cause ah goat it aw, the very fuckin same treatment fae ma auld man n it did me nae fuckin herm at aw. Cruel tae be kind, like they say. N ah'm livin proof thit it's the best wey. Ah mean, ye nivir see me in any fuckin bother wi the polis, no since way back. Learnt ma fuckin lesson: ah keep ma nose clean n ah gie they cunts a wide berth. Aw ah ask ootay life is a few bevvies, the fitba n the occasional ride.

That makes ays think bit: what's it gaunny be like ridin her if she's no goat any fuckin legs . . . So we gits up the casualty n this doaktir cunt's gaun oan aboot me bein in shock n ah'm thinkin aboot the fitba n if these cunts've scored awready ah'll be in fuckin shock awright. Ah turns tae the boy n goes, − Hi mate, ken me n her, ken like whin wir the gither?

Cunt wisnae gittin ma drift.

− Ken in bed likes? The cunt nods. − See if she's no goat any fuckin legs, will ah still be able tae cowp it likes?

− Sorry? this cunt goes.

Thick as fuck. A fuckin doaktir this is n aw. Thought ye hud tae huv fuckin brains tae dae that joab. − Ah'm talkin aboot oor sex life, ah tell um.

− Well, assuming your wife survives, your sex life should be normal, the cunt says, lookin at ays like ah wis some kind ay radge.

− Well, ah goes, − that's ah bit ay fuckin good news, cause it

54 wisnae fuckin well normal before! No unless ye call a ride every three fuckin months or something like that normal, n that's no what ah fuckin well call normal.

So thair ah wis, tryin tae watch the fuckin game oan the waitin room telly. Nae bevvy or nowt, n aw they radges hasslin ays wi forms n questions n the fuckin bairns playin up gaun oan aboot 'is she awright', n 'when ur wi gaun hame' n aw that shite. Ah fuckin well warned the wee cunts aboot nippin ma heid n aw: see whin ah git youse hame, ah telt them.

Tell yis one thing fir nowt though, whin she's oot ay that hoaspital, see if she cannae dae things aroond the hoose, ah'm fuckin offski. Too fuckin right ya cunt. Lookin eftir a fat cunt wi nae fuckin legs! That will be fuckin shinin bright! It wis her ain fault as well, the fuckin fat cunt. Fuckin things up fir me like that. No thit the game wis anything tae write hame aboot mind you, another fuckin nil-nil draw but, eh.

ROBERT CRAWFORD

Harasser

Eyes fixed
clear polyurethane
headlights
following you home
down a single-track

twisting
between high hedges,
up behind you
closer sometimes,
revving,

then dropping back
in dark rain,
fog-lamps
searching you out,
knowing exactly

where
and just how much pressure
on the gas
would be needed,
if it came to that.

ROBERT CRAWFORD

Anstruther

Here the great presbyterian minister
With his lifeboat and memorial lighthouse

Sails with the captain of many clippers
Towards the Salutation Bar.

Herring gulls take off. Terns loop down to us striding
On slime-green steppingstones over the dreel

Under a clear, bespectacled sky
Crowstepped with masonic symbols.

Where the Beggar's Benison met to measure their pricks
On a special platter, we stand and stare up at the stars

Near the electrician's. They look so close
They should be catching lobsters and called

Not the Plough but Breadwinner III,
Shearwater of Cellardyke, North Carr Lightship,

Morning Ray, Fisher of Men.
High above piers and long breakwaters

They trawl dour, intergalactic North Seas,
Making pantiles sparkle and cornfields with tubular stooks

Harvested in farmtouns beyond Anstruther
Wink in their great moderator's eye

Overseeing his congregation
As they sing in a tethered boat that is bobbing

Down and up, gently
Up and down.

Mee

She kept phoning us up before she died
To say how much she wanted you to have them,

Deep lilac, maxims, tables, articles.
She had no children. They were out of date,

The Earth is Always Moving, Heredity,
Herschel, The Man Who Listed the Great Stars.

The Boy Who Saved his Family, Tortoises,
Milan Cathedral, Engines and their Ways,

She forgot everything
Except that you were going to be born.

We lied, and told her that we'd like them for you,
So here they are, piled in the vestibule,

Wee girls at rockpools in the 1920s,
How a Thermos Works, Flags of the World

That should be bagged and binned, but becomes yours—
A hangover, a canny, defunct smell

Of Lysol, or one loved, defective gene
Inhibiting your signature, her hand

Cursively not there, but still writing for you,
'The affectionate friend of children, Arthur Mee.'

The Sophisticate

I am a tall, mid-Western professor
Arrived in Paris for my very first time

Aware it's a city of the imagination
Yet solid as this kerb in Montparnasse.

Patisseries, deep spinnach roulades, sex,
Dark-varnished shelves of petites tartes oignons—

I buy a hat, a small cigar, and then
In the middle of the great colloquium

When I leap up to give my keynote speech
I clearly see its thirty numbered pages

Unscuffed, kept tidy by a paperclip,
Locked in the third drawer down, left far behind me

In Iowa, or dour Lincoln, Nebraska,
Or Second Pond, Joesville, or Junction Gulch.

THE WASTING OF OLD ENGLISH SPEECH AND HOW A NEW WAS GOT

By Alasdair Gray

Lord Finook sometimes had to boil his cottages – to get the cottagers out.

IVOR CUTLER

William, boss of Normandy, belonged to a fourth or fifth generation of Scandinavian pirates who had forced themselves as a military aristocracy upon much of England, France and Italy. Being closely related, their strongest chiefs always had genealogical excuses for claiming a neighbour's territory, and at land-grabbing nobody beat boss William. He was strong, brave, clever, patient, greedy, violent and revengeful – a nasty man, but soldiers who fought for him and survived were sure of victory and loot. Like some others of Viking blood he felt entitled to the English throne. Hearing that the English national assembly of wise men had elected Harold, an Englishman, to the job, William prepared to invade. First he persuaded his barons to follow him, for the feudal code gave him no right to order them overseas against unthreatening Christians, and conquest would be hard. For twelve years Harold had already ruled England peacefully and well as the previous king's chief minister. That was why the leaders of England's mingled Celtic, Saxon and Danish communities had crowned him. William told the Norman barons that he could double their estates in France by the addition of English ones. They believed him. In a Europe with hardly any international money system he raised a lot of money, and built a fleet, and hired mercenary troops from French neighbours who might otherwise have attacked Normandy when he left.

60   In 1066 the army of another warrior who wanted England landed in the north, and while Harold was defeating it William invaded the south and began laying waste. Turning a peopled, productive land into wilderness was as common a military tactic in the 11th century as the 20th. It made rulers who cared for their people fight invaders while the invaders were still enthusiastic. Harold's private soldiers were mostly farmers and ploughmen, not trained mercenaries. Most of his officers were landlords with fighting experience, not hereditary fighters for land. Harold was killed, the English beaten, the nobles who fought for him fled. William set fire to south London. The remaining southern nobles and bishops proclaimed him king, hoping he would leave them their property and positions. They were mistaken. He began building a great tower in London which became the Anglo–Norman capital. Across the land his barons began the other bleak stone fortresses with dungeons in the basements from which the English would be controlled for the next three or four centuries. For five years William kept crushing English risings in the south, the east, the west (where they were aided by their old enemies the Welsh) but especially in the north, where they were helped by the Scots and Danes. In the north he bribed the Danes to leave, then burned towns and villages, killing resisters or driving them over the Scottish border. He carefully destroyed homes, harvests, cattle and farming tools, making a famine to kill all survivors. The north never troubled him again. Half a century later, the sixty miles northward of York was still unpeopled desert.

Official gossip called William *the Conqueror*. They should have called him the Waster. Even in peacetime he laid waste, getting a hunting park the size of a small county by clearing from it people, farms and religious settlements. His five years of spectacular violence at last forced peace on the land whose peace he had destroyed, but he could only keep England now by making permanent the army he had used to grab it. He did so by a vast confiscation of productive soil. The defeat of widespread English resistance had killed or driven abroad all the big landlords and many small ones. He evicted others, letting the most servile keep a small part of their estate in return for the rest and a promise to serve him always. William could now give his poorest mercenary land with a village on it, his biggest supporters and nearest relations estates of a hundred manors and more. He kept the biggest estates, and where he lacked troops to overawe the natives he evicted the natives and made a game reserve. He ensured that the estates of his biggest landlords (potential rivals) were in far-apart pieces: some on the dangerous borders of Wales and Scotland, some in the counties near London. This meant they could not swiftly unite their troops against him. To efficiently locate and tax his subjects he made an itinerant bureaucracy name, number, measure and record every estate, property and owner. All England was now under the martial law of a widespread army he could mobilize any time.

In those days the bishop of Rome, another Gregory, invited Christian kings to do him honour as their earthly overlord. The German emperor did so but William refused. He replaced nearly every English bishop and abbot with a Norman French clergyman who paid him the same homage as his barons did, communicated only through him with the papacy, made no big decisions without his consent. Having made himself as complete a master of church and state as did the eighth Henry five centuries later, William spent most of his remaining years in Normandy from where he wasted towns and countryside in warfare with the king of France.

Primo Levi says there is no violence against people without violence against language. Douglas, in a small book called *The Norman Conquest and British Historians*, says, 'Perhaps the two greatest achievements of mediaeval England were Anglo-Saxon vernacular literature and Anglo-Norman executive administration.' Perhaps. The second achievement destroyed the first. The livelihood of the English now depended on them understanding the orders of confident foreign despots who, like all that sort, acted as if the natives were mostly fools or villains. 'Do you think

62 I'm an *Englishman*?' was a Norman French way of saying, 'Do you think I'm a fool?' *Villain* was originally Norman French for a villager who tilled the soil: the most essential kind of worker, but despicable from the viewpoint of a military aristocrat. So in the new language the English made by blending the words of their masters with their own, *villainous* meant *criminal*. At the end of the eighth century Great Alfred had given England a continuous vernacular history. He sent abbeys throughout the land an up-to-date factual chronicle of events since the Roman conquest, as far as they were known, asking that each year the abbeys add to their copy a list of events befalling the kingdom. It was part of his plan to help the English read and write in their own culture, to which the clerical among them could add Latin. These chronicles were continued for over three centuries, but gradually fall silent after the Conquest, when William ordered the church grammar schools to start teaching in French. By the twelfth century the invaders had persuaded the English priests, merchants and small gentry that their history and literature were best forgotten, their language was a speech of the ignorant. The last purely English bishop had been deposed because 'he was a superannuated English idiot who spoke no French'.

England was now half of an empire split in two by a channel of the sea, an empire whose military landlords fought to add Wales and Scotland to their northern estates, all France to their southern ones. Their attacks on Wales united that land in a resistance which, successful at first, inspired Welsh bards to make poetry still recited and enjoyed by Welsh readers. The first Spanish epic, *El Cid*, was from the twelfth century, when singers and fabulists also began making the first literature of Mediterranean France. A century later Dante wrote *The Divine Comedy*, a Christian epic as great as Homer's and Virgil's. In three hundred years of Welsh, Spanish, French, Italian vernacular excellence a few poignant sentences in old English lament for lost learning, describe a scholar's tearful joy that a book by Bede still exists. The Anglo-French meanwhile wrote laws, state annals and hunting manuals. Their imaginative writing (anti-clerical satire and fabulous Arthurian history) was got from the Celts of Wales and Brittany.

Which does not mean intelligent life ended in England for three hundred years. No kings who came after William could be so absolute. The church got partly free of them, then the barons. Wasted ground was resettled. People, trades and towns increased – they would have done so had the Normans been repelled. Prospering tradesmen and merchants could pay high taxes, so kings protected them from the barons, big towns won free of military landlords. Some farmers got partly free too, paying rent in coin instead of labour. The king, church, towns, landlords were now linked by codes and contracts which made understanding these a full-time job. Big colleges added law to their curriculums. Then trade, crusades and pilgrimages brought Islamic writing to Europe. It contained developments in Arabic science with work by Aristotle and other Greek thinkers lost to the West. The church colleges spread word of them. Translation, commentary, subtle ideas now seemed adventurous things, repulsive only to the conservative and timid. Western universities expanded like boom towns on the American frontier. Life there was quarrelsome, democratic, sometimes murderous; but the coarsely gowned and often barefoot fellows who jostled sons of nobility in the lecture halls were seeking knowledge, not gold. Oxford housed students from England, Scotland, Wales, Normandy and Gascony. Roger Bacon, Duns Scotus, William of Ockham taught in Oxford: brave thinkers who lectured and wrote in Latin.

By the fourteenth century the French people had more nobility than they could bear. The nobles thought battles a traditional, legal way to get fame and property, a natural extension of combats which were their education in childhood and sports in peacetime. They were proud of their politeness to fallen enemies of their own rank. Unhorsed in fights that killed many foot soldiers, protected by armour a dagger could hardly pierce, a captured knight might soon be dining with his captor and his captor's wife in a castle like his own, suffering

64   only some bruises and a rueful awareness of the large ransom his estate would pay for his release. But the cost was mostly paid by his peasants, and plunder was a legal right of the higher nobility when their supplies ran short. In France, Europe's most fertile and cultivated land, the tillers of it suffered more and more hunger. Alas, only nobles had the technology to destroy nobles. A full set of armour was then the equivalent of a twentieth-century tank. From a wholly French view the most superfluous nobles were obviously the Anglo-French.

Warfare started which at last drove these from their French estates and made them wholly English, but for over a hundred years they could not believe it because they kept winning battles. Mainland Britain was a safe place to retreat to, a good recruiting ground to attack from. Their English estates could not yield enough men to fight a war for five generations, so they raised regiments from the free townsmen and free farmers by offering pay, loot, and ransoms of captured French. They urged them to use the longbow, a new invention which enabled strong men to shoot arrows through armour. Middle-class tradesmen and yeomen could handle it, being muscular as peasants and well fed as gentry. Noble commanders spoke to them in English, as if such soldiers were almost their equals. For centuries the nobles (like German and Russian nobles before Napoleon's wars) had spoken French to show their superiority: a bad tactic when ordering Englishmen to kill Frenchmen in France. The middle-class troops and their longbows were effective. England's kings and barons kept regaining nominal lordship of French land which paid them little or nothing. Their footsoldiers got coins, a loot of fine clothing, ornaments, household goods, and a new confidence in their speech. Froissart, historian of that time, was astonished by the arrogance low-ranking English showed to Frenchmen of every rank. When these soldiers returned to their trades and small properties in England, they also spoke more directly to their rulers. Then a worse disease than warfare made every social rank talk straight to each other.

There were perhaps four million English when the Black

Death reached them in 1349. By the end of the century 65
epidemics had killed between a third and half. People of every
rank died, but the loss of a third of the labourers wrought
biggest changes – their work fed the rest. They too discovered
some freedom of choice, for despite government efforts to keep
down wages those who could afford it still bid for their labour.
The building of great cathedrals and palaces stopped. Chronicles
filled with laments for the terrible greed of the poor, a sign of
social improvement where wealth is unequally shared. Debate
grew widespread, everywhere people arguing what was due to
them as nobility, Christians, citizens, householders, Englishmen,
spokesmen for a trade, craft, closed shop or open union. All
sorts of English were about to enter the public house of a new
literate speech.

This speech was no longer the speech of Caedmon and Alfred.
The English no longer (like folk in other lands) made words
for complex things by linking short ones, so that guilt-doing
became *gyltendum*, the-world-shaping became *woruldgesceafte*.
Three centuries of national and local bossing in French had
ground the Anglo-Saxon-Danish word-hoard down small and
kept it small, leaving curt little words which did, and still do,
most of the hard work in English: *a the and for or but me she
he you it that those these them what when*; and verbs showing
tense by changing their start, middle or end like *is/was see/saw
think/thought keep/kept*; and verbs which were useful nouns and
vice versa, like *work love milk stick*; and adjectives which could
be nouns, like *fat good salt red kind*; even *light*, a word which
toils discreetly and well as noun, adjective and verb. But such
words no longer connected and supported big combinations of
themselves. The big words had been mostly got from the French
of landlords, clergy, lawyers and schoolteachers, had different
spellings from the short words and different pronunciations:
even though the native English spoke them with flatter mouths
than the French.

Thus, since the fourteenth century, English vocabulary has
looked like a garden of turf and herbs in which grow eye-catching

66 flowers from a richer climate. Looking back through a sentence (this sentence) for words of French origin, I immediately see *immediately*, *origin* and *sentence*. If I hated French things I could replace *immediately* by *at once* and gain terseness, but to replace *origin* I would need to turn *words of French origin* into *words got long ago from the French*, which is wordier. And there is now no easily understood group of English words from the Anglo-Saxon which could mean *sentence*. Not all French Latinate words are longer than Anglo-Saxon equivalents: *centre/middle, comprehension/understanding* are equal lengths, but the first of each pair seems politer, grander, the result of dearer educations. Walter Scott pointed out that slaughter converted Saxon pigs (or swine) into French pork. Of course! Haute Cuisine had raised it to the landlord's table. The ease with which English words can be split into polite/rich and homely/poor is (apart from the English political constitution) the worst legacy of the Norman conquest. Whenever the wealthy in England gain more power they spread the idea that the king's or queen's English is theirs, that poorer speech ties the rest to commonplace objects and feelings, so they cannot think deeply or talk with authority. England's best writing proves that false. 'Dust to dust and ashes to ashes,' spoken over a grave, offers a profounder thought than 'the transience of human existence,' and only a bad writer would use a phrase like the last. The translators of the Bible into English deliberately used an English so plain that the only grand words are Hebrew and Latin names. Chaucer, Shakespeare, Thomas Hardy used and even invented big grand words, but used them to add force or exactness or an exciting image to the common speech. They succeeded. They were popular.

But the new English of Chaucer's century was not exactly ours. This shows the main verbal differences:

Whan that Aprill with his shoures soote
The droghte of March hath perced to the root . . .

Whan (when) rhymes more with *swan* than with *can*.　　67

Shoures (showers). The first four letters rhyme with *hour*, the last two with *yes*, but with the *s* said more lightly.

Soote (sweet) should be pronounced delicately and Frenchly with protruded lips, the final *e* said very short, so that it sounds very different from *sooty*.

Droughte (drought). The *gh* is pronounced like the last two letters of Bach or a highland loch: the final *e* as in *soote*, but shorter still, as the rhythm leaves less room for it.

Perced (pierced). The first four letters sound like the first four in *Percy*, the last two like the last two in *bedded*.

Roote (root) rhymes with *soote*.

This English had an almost Italianate lilt and flow from sounding the short *e* at the end of many words that have dropped it, and at the end of words like inspir*ed* where we no longer pronounce it, and in the use of *es* for a plural ending. The lilt was ballasted by that harsh *gh* which is still a conspicuous part of many English words, though nowadays only pronounced in parts of Scotland.

Please read on.

THE ALEXANDRIAN LIBRARY, PART II: THE RETURN OF THE BOOK

By Don Paterson

The level blue gaze of the lovely librarian
has wrestled your own to the floor,
half an hour of her husky insistence finally
coaxing from you, like a long-buried skelf,
the real reason you can't seem to talk to your father.
Beneath the professional concern, you detect
something akin to desire;
though she must let you work, now, and leaves
with a quick little squeeze of the shoulder,
sexually neutral, but somehow prolonged enough
not to oblige you to write off the much-refined
after-hours stockroom scenario
as wishful thinking entirely.
You keep listening, till the bristling efficiency
of her nylons criss-crossing inside her starched whites
has shushed the whole place back to silence.

The tip of your ballpoint is weeping black ink
over the snowy divan of the notepad,
as if it were dreaming incontinently
of the glories to come, but this is the real thing,
and as such, it will get the full treatment:
the thirty-seven classical stations of courtly love,
the hymeneal rites of Byzantine complexity,
the Song and the Book and the Film of the Act,
its magnification, discussion, rehearsal,
its almost-indefinite postponement:

for no one has had this idea before—
how you will cherish their tear-stricken faces
the morning you fly the stained sheets from the window!

While shifting your weight to one buttock, silently
breaking the seal on an odourless fart,
you split open the vacuum of black Costa Rica;
the smell of it, capric and deeply provocative,
swims up and wafts itself under your nose
like a flick-knife. You refresh your favourite mug,
the blue Smarties job with the handle still on.
The ghost of your hangover thunders away
(like a train; this should go without saying)
into the featureless steppes, its heart set
on magnetic north; in a couple of hours
it will dock in a small town just short of the Circle,
known dimly, if anyone knows it at all,
for its lead-mines, a dangerous method of throat-singing
and an ardent liqueur, distilled from white turnips
with the taste and appearance of liquid acetylene
and its consequent, utterly perfect effacement
of perceptual borders; two fingers of this stuff
and everything turns into everything else.
At midnight, you tattoo the Horseman's Word
on the back of your wrist with a pin and a biro
then slip into blissful insentience.
In the morning, excluding the state of your trousers,
it seems there's no damage to pay;
just a stunned vacuity, furred at the edges,
as if you looked out at the world through a big hole
someone had smashed in your living-room window.
A little confused, you spend an hour failing
to scrub the word SPONG from your wrist, then set out
for a leisurely tour of the second-hand book-stalls.
Around midday, you notice the demon of accidie
perched on the steeple, yawning contagiously;

70   you make plans to deal with him, considering, in turn,
a propitiatory nap, the dubbed Polish game-show,
even, roguishly, the hair of the dog.
On the last stroke of noon, he lets fly with the ice-pick
you will wear in your head for a fortnight.

You've developed the habit, at this hour, of randomly
lifting a book from the shelves;
here, there are nothing but books about Art,
that is to say, books with just pictures;
Monday was Twombly, yesterday Watteau,
this afternoon, Balthus: brought to the light,
the brilliant plan you have unconsciously nursed
for the past fifteen minutes turns out to be merely
the prospect of having a wank before teatime.
You will swither luxuriously over a choice:
to swan up, or not, to the top of the building,
then the one extra flight to the glassy enclosure
you share with the brown-winged, probationary angels,
to settle back under the skylight, with Balthus
spread out on the tiles, while the pine-scented ozone
comes walloping in through the vent.
(An atom-sized blowfly goes zipping erratically
across the white field of your conscience, too small
for conclusive identification.)

In the stillness, you make out the delicate jangle
of tiny chimes, thin rods of crystal and amethyst
threaded on silk; to play them, it strikes you,
would feel just like stroking a feather;
it is a universe, advanced in its state
of chromatic decay, gently disbanding
in the long pole of sunlight that falls from the ceiling,
fixing your jotter exactly. Right now,
if literature were quantum mechanics
you'd be just a sniff from the theory of everything—

one breezy reckoning on the back of a beermat
and that would be that, fuck Einstein. As it is,
with the silence now thickened enough to be workable
and the words ranged like tools on an infinite shadow-board,
each one on the tip of your tongue (i.e. *ranine*),
it is almost time to begin.

The room looks to have lost all faith in itself
– a good sign, you know – as if seconds before
the wall had sprung back from the floor like a pop-up book
to be fingered by God, his hand bracing your shoulder
to steady you as he yanks at the tab
that sticks out of your head, making your writing arm
jerk up and down in big squiggles.
Now everything hangs in the balance,
as if the whole world could be brought into being
by the fact of its clear elocution, as if
the planet now hovered and hummed on the brink
of the great bimillennial switch of polarities
that wiped out the dinosaurs, kick-started the ice-age,
knocked up the virgin, deflected the moon
quietly out of its course.

Now the last touch – your new toy, '*Infraworlds—
For the Gentle Enhancement of Personal Space*',
a series of ambient soundtracks designed
to be superimposed over absolute silence,
since virtually nothing is on them.
You have *Scottish Renaissance; Café Voltaire*
and *Library*; though, as usual, you plump for
Buenos Aires, Early Evening, 1896,
firk out the cassette from its soft pastel cover
and jiggle it into your Walkman.
At first, there seems to be nothing but tape-hiss
though it seeps imperceptibly into the white rush
of steam from a kettle of maté;

72 through the half-opened casement, a spatter of horse-traffic,
the shudders and yawns of a distant bandoneon;
from a bar on the opposite side of the street,
over the blink of small glasses, two men
discuss metaphysics, or literature;
from previous listenings you know, in an hour or so,
the talk will come round to the subject of women,
and then to one girl in particular;
and end with the phthisical freshing of metal
(you will whack up the volume for this bit),
a short protestation that ends in a gurgle,
screak of a chair-leg on ironwood parquet
and your man spanking off down an alley.
Till then, you will work.

The new poem is coming along like a dream:
this is the big one, the one that will finally
consolidate everything. It is the usual,
but different: a series of localized, badly-lit,
paradigmatic atrocities seen from a train
at the hour between dusk and oblivion,
but – O his audacity! – rendered as *pastoral*:
the sensitive, paranoid, derelict romance,
the only response that is humanly adequate
now, at this point at the end of the century;
the song that the rest will all find themselves singing
too late, and the words will be yours. You will sue.
It is perfect in length, while your witless coevals,
all keen, when the big flash goes off, to be caught
in the apposite gesture, have spent the last five years
conscientiously failing to finish the epic
or grinding and polishing four lines of nothing
in the desperate hope that the planet will somehow
fall into its transparent curves.

In the poem you appear as a poet, a real one,
with a book out, and two or three gigs in the diary
though neither the taxman, your shrink nor the Gas Board
is having it. Last week, at the manse
for the cosy wee pep-talk arranged by your mother,
the minister, somewhere between the sweet sherry
and the meat-paste and cucumber sandwiches,
leant across, laid his fat paw on your shoulder
and whispered *for fuck's sake, get real, son.*
The train in the poem is rushing you home
as if it remembered what you had forgotten
to water or feed or lock up or turn off;
perhaps you will find the whole house has been stolen,
in its place, just the transom you failed to snib shut;
and what parcel of bloodsuckers, slugs and winged beetles
will the late second post have chucked up on the
    doormat—
the summons, the x-ray results, the week's notice
of the warranty sale, the genuine death threats
from the jealous, the recently badly-reviewed,
that mad bloke you met at the workshop?
Now enter the bit-player you think you remember
from the black-and-white Carry-On films, though in
    your poems
invariably cast as the louche psychopomp—
widow's peak, wall-eye, BO, the lot.
A full set of obsolete dental equipment
fills his breast-pocket; trailing a fingertip
over the tight row of flame-burs and stylets,
he pauses over a mildew-pocked speculum
with which he will take all the time in the world
to find everything wrong with your ticket.
You are describing his hand falling down on your
    shoulder
    like something to do with a hawk or a lobster
        when his hand falls down on your shoulder

in precisely the manner you failed to describe,
and somehow the big switch is made.

The lens flies back, offering a view
of yourself from above, then the two of you, stiff
in a caption of light, the last in a series
of bright rooms, some empty, some spartanly furnished
with their little vignette, like an unfinished strip-cartoon
of which you are clearly the punchline;
then plunges away through the abstracted night
till the train is no more than the pulsating hyphen
in London-Brighton, a jittery point
of no ascertainable hue or dimension
that resolves as the glint in his good eye,
has a half-hearted stab at a twinkle, then fails.
And there, on the page, is the lovely librarian,
the coffee so vividly drawn you could smell it
were it not for the audible whine of his oxters,
his skidmarks and forty years' Kensitas
that admits of no other alternative.

They have let you go home. You sit in the dark,
count slowly up to fifty
then switch on that absolute moron, the anglepoise:
with a sputter of wet wood, the back of your head
explodes in slow motion; through the axehead of sparks
come the horror-waves no one has ever conveyed
without buggering with the typography:
your writing is almost entirely illegible,
and you will never know, since you cannot remember
whether you'd sat in the train or the library,
if it was the page, or your hand shaking.

Envoi

Someone appears to be using your mouth
to scream through: you shut it abruptly,

oddly relieved to discover the neighbours
pounding the wall, in concern or annoyance;
unfortunately, your house is semi-detached,

that is the gable-end, this is the first floor,
    and, with a bang and a fizz
here is a door where no door was before
    and where the door was no door is

CROSSING THE BORDER

By Shena Mackay

Flora had never been so far south. She was driving past sari shops, silk wholesalers, sweetshops and sweatshops, restaurants and jewellers, through a low-rise landscape broken by spires and temples and mosques, in Sunday afternoon traffic puffing out bouquets of January gloom. Her own secondhand Metro was fuelled by a mixture of anticipation and doubt. Long streets of stuccoed terraced houses curved away on either side of the road, and then the red brick pagoda of a Tesco Superstore reared up and blue galvanised warehouses and DIY emporia, and now she was in the half-timbered hinterland where London ebbs into the pampas grass and mock-Tudor of the edge of Kent, taking the wrong turning at a roundabout.

When Flora had left home, the dark bobbles of the plane trees in the Square where she lived were draggling like trimmings of frowsty curtains in a sky of mushroom soup. Now, as the road petered out into a rutted track, and she stopped the car, the sun licked through the glutinous grey, revealing streaks of pale blue glaze; and linking a gold necklace of dazzling puddles. Across a small field, behind the bare twigs of oak trees, Flora could see what must be the backs of the houses in the road she had missed, Bourne Avenue. At the field's edge, a single black angler was fishing a pond encircled with barbed wire where white geese swam, and two booted and anoraked women walked past with seven or eight dogs leaping between them, and Flora stepped out into a mild composty wind and locked the car. Elders and wooden fence posts were emerald green with winter. She picked her way over gravel and mud, telling herself that ten minutes more would make no difference to Great Uncle Lorimer after all these years. To her left, in a thin tangled wood, here and there the massive trunk of an oak, felled to some ten feet in height, sported a crown of new pale antlers. Flora took them as a sign that her quest would be successful, for she was, in a sense, seeking her own roots, tracing a branch of her family tree; and there was a tape recorder in the bag on her shoulder.

Her chief interest lay in her late great-uncle Laurence, the poet, and she was hoping that his brother Lorimer would give her insights into and anecdotes from the shared childhood of two sons of the manse who had taken such different paths. Flora, like her great-uncles, was among those of the large Looney family who had dropped the second 'o' from their name, defying the world's determination thence to style them Looney or Lonely. Uncle Lorimer had reverted to the original, for reasons of his own. Flora, whose father was a poet of a different kind, a corduroy-jacketed and much-married journeyman, had determined to write the biography of Laurence Loney, who had died alone in a trailer park in Nevada, and she had got as far as her title, *Tumbleweed and Whin*, which encapsulated the unhappy, contradictory character of the author of *Poor Pink Trash* and *Behind The Scones At The Tattoo*. Like Laurence, she was moved by ephemera and junk and saw the poignancy of broken turquoise beads in the dust, eternity in a plastic flower and the human condition in the brittle pink Little Princess Vanity Set in the supermarket, whose tiny mirror flashed a fragment of dream. The bleached bones of a bird or a skull in the heather spoke to her too, as plaintively as a peewit or the pale torso of a lost Barbie doll.

The tips of birches made a rosy haze in the distance against a sky growing colder and Flora could hear the chilly sound of running water and, squelching into the wood, she discovered a brown swift stream carrying dead leaves and little gnarled alder fruits between its steep banks. A middle-aged man with a red setter was approaching and, surmising that he was not a murderer, Flora called out,

'Is there a bridge across this stream?'

'Stream? This is the Ravensbourne river!'

A stalwart local historian, Flora recognised, as the dog scrambled into the water, splashing against the current in a whirligig of red feathery ears and tail and radiant droplets, and the man followed it upstream. Flora returned to the path and walked on, encountering several more of these unfriendly, not-quite-country-folk, until she found herself on the verge of a Pick Your Own smallholding where strawberry plants huddled in sodden spangled furrows of black plastic, at a makeshift shelter of corrugated tin and polythene where the strawberries were weighed in the summer. Time to turn back, but there was something shimmering golden and dazzling at the end of the track, with bright flashes of moving colours.

It was a heap, a low mountain, of shining straw mucked out from stables, glinting gilt and copper and brass in the sun as Flora drew near, its stalks clogged with horse manure, and on its peak stood a cockerel, red–gold and viridescent. Guineafowl, turkeys, cocks and hens and ornamental pheasants pecked about on the pungent slopes and ridges of the magic midden, astonishing and entrancing Flora with their display of drooping shot-silk tailfeathers, yellow chinoiserie, scarlet and coral combs and cloisonné plumage.

While she had been wandering in that strange landscape, Flora had been able to forget herself, and to flinch only slightly when her rebuffed smiles fell like dying butterflies into the mud, but the mirror in the car brought her abruptly back to Flora Loney, aged twenty-seven, wind-smudged and damp, lips chafed, blue eyes watering, fair hair in clumps of straw on the shoulders of her coat, black ankle boots stained and black tights speckled and a smear of dirt across one unusually pink cheekbone. Yes, she looked inescapably like Flora, blurred, anxious, untidy and late, with new footwear ruined by a careless impulse. If Great-Uncle Lorimer had not been expecting her, she would have gone straight home, carrying with her the picture of those exotic birds on the golden dunghill as sufficient adventure for one day. She reversed along the track, splashing a sullen couple in woolly hats, negotiated the turning into Bourne Avenue and found a parking space. Flora walked up the path on her long black legs under her short black coat as nervously as a little girl going to a party, with her tape recorder in her bag, clutching a paper cone of orange spray carnations.

The house looked ordinary enough, Edwardian, double-fronted, with dull green paint and windows looking out on to wintry shrubs and the tips of bulbs, but what had she expected, a bunch of balloons bobbing on the gate, a bucket of whitewash balanced on the porch? She took a deep breath and pushed the bell, heard its tired voice in the interior, and waited, contemplating an umbrella like an injured fruitbat. Footsteps shuffled, and the door was opened by an old woman in purple pom-pommed slippers, with her hair piled in an elaborate confection of peroxide peaks and swirls on top of her head, circles of rouge on white powdered cheeks and a crimson mouth in which her own lips were lost somewhere. Giggling with relief, Flora said, 'I can see I've come to the right house!'

'What do you mean?'

'The Home For Retired Clowns.'

'Next door,' said the woman, shutting her own in Flora's face, which burst into flames of embarrassment and guilt.

Flora could have wept at her own ill-judged verbal custard pie. 'Me and my big mouth,' she thought, fishing in her pocket for a stub of lip salve and applying it to her wide, frayed lips, She could no more make amends than she could have eaten her words at the dinner party the night before, when she had remarked, 'a fettucine worse than death' as her hostess put down the dish. After that, everything, including the soufflé that followed, had fallen rather flat. Flora was almost at the gate when she heard,

'Miss!'

She turned, ready to attempt an apology.

'I doubt if they'll take you. Why don't you try a different career? Apply for one of those government re-training schemes?'

'Yes, thanks. I might do that. Good idea,' Flora was bleating as the door snapped shut again.

The name on the gate was Grimsby Lodge. Grimaldi House was indeed the house next door. But the false clownesse had been nearer the mark than she knew. A few years earlier, Flora had been one of only two students, in a class of thirty-five, who had failed to graduate with a degree in Circus Skills. Just one more smallish shame in a lifetime of fumbled catches and dropped opportunities. How right Daddy had been to suggest that Flora was a little unbalanced even to contemplate the high wire, and how smug he had been when she had fallen off. Since she had flunked Circus Skills, she had seen former classmates coining it in from the crowd in Covent Garden, and once, broke and desperate, behind with the rent, Flora had set up with her juggling balls, on someone else's pitch, only to be pelted from the Piazza. Her fellow-failure, a young woman named Ziggy Deville, with whom Flora was superficially friendly, now had her own column on a newspaper which paid her vast sums of money to write about her hangovers, discarded diets, disastrous love-life and the drug-related deaths of her flatmates.

A sad-faced visitor was leaving Grimaldi House as Flora arrived and he held the front door open for her, admitting her to the hall, where she tinkled the ceramic handbell that stood under a vase of beige silk roses on the polished table, next to the visitors' book. Flora glanced at the page, hoping to recognise some illustrious name, and saw that somebody had drawn a smiley face by way of signature, and waited apprehensively, inhaling a potpourri of late-afternoon ennui, tea in plastic beakers and air freshener. A portrait of the great Grimaldi hung on the wall, opposite a garish and rather tactless print of a clown with downturned mouth and a teardrop oozing from his painted eye. Televisions rumbled behind doors, cutlery clashed in a distant steel sink. A small woman of Far-Eastern mien, in a pink overall, appeared.

'Can I help you?'

'Oh, yes, thank you. I've come to see my great-uncle. Lorimer Loney. He's expecting me. I wrote.'

The women stared at Flora.

'Looney the Clown,' Flora added helpfully.

'Oh dear. If you'd like to just take a seat in the visitors' lounge.'

A white door was closed behind Flora. She sat on the chintz sofa wondering what the pink-overalled woman had meant: *if* Flora just took a seat, would Great-Uncle Lorimer be wheeled in to her in a chair like the one she had seen folded in the hall; would she be led into a roomful of clowns in full motley and be expected to pick out the right one? She hadn't seen Looney since she was three and had to be carried screaming back to her seat after she had rushed into the ring to batter with her tiny fists the clown who had tipped a bucket of yellow paint down Looney's trousers. Would she just be left sitting here until she was old enough to be wheeled away herself? Not daring to try the door in case it was locked, Flora combated her panic by deep breathing. Nobody knew she was here. She had told nobody of her mission that afternoon. She tried to concentrate on the hand-stitched Serenity Prayer on the wall, but it reminded her of a friend who had lost a toe in the throes of a Charismatic service in the Brompton Road, and she turned to a signed poster of the Cottle Sisters Circus. Grimaldi House was, she knew, a benevolent institution founded by a famous circus family and maintained by voluntary contributions and fund-raising activities. Flora recalled seeing a minibus without wheels in the front garden. The residents of Grimaldi House weren't going anywhere it seemed. She began to worry about the woman in the pink overall, and wonder if she were a prisoner too. A Filipina child-prostitute, tricked into a fake marriage, and held as a suburban slave, possibly even a sex-slave, in a house of dotard clowns.

Was it her duty to help the woman to escape? Ziggy Deville would have known what to do, and she could expose the whole

82 racket in her paper. If only she had a mobile, she could call Ziggy now. Except that she'd probably be asleep or too hungover to speak or in bed with somebody, or dead or something. Flora heard the desolate buzzing and thumping of a vacuum cleaner, such a bleak sound on a Sunday afternoon, and an old man droning out, 'If you don't want the whelks, don't muck 'em abaht', over and over again, until Flora felt lost on a timeless foreshore of grey unwanted whelkshells ceaselessly shifting with the tide. She was about to try the door, when it opened and a tall, fair woman in a brown and beige jacquard dress came in.

'I'm Mrs Endersby. Sit down again won't you, my dear. That's better. I'm afraid I've got some rather sad news for you. Mr Loney slipped away from us in the early hours this morning.'

'How?' said Flora, dazedly picturing a clown sliding like a shadow under a sash window into the pre-dawn darkness and shinning down a drainpipe.

'He was expecting me. I wrote. I really need to talk to him. I'm his brother's official biographer, sort of.'

'I'm afraid he just couldn't hang on any longer, dear. He was already very frail, and an infection in somebody of his age . . . of course the sixty cigarettes a day for all those years, until he came to us, had taken their toll . . .'

Flora gazed at Mrs Endersby. It was the first time she had actually seen somebody wearing that dress advertised on the back pages of tabloid Sunday supplements, with always-smart gilt-effect buttons and matching belt-buckle trim. She realized that she was sitting on her flowers.

'Am I being thick?' she asked. 'I mean, are you trying to tell me that Great-Uncle Lorimer is dead?'

'I'm so sorry, my dear. I would have hoped that somebody might have saved you a journey – some of the relatives have collected his bits and pieces, and the gentlemen from Messrs Chappell are in charge of the Arrangements. They gave one of our little family a lovely send-off recently, with a baby elephant pulling the hearse. Perhaps you saw it on Newsroom South East?

Oh, no, you wouldn't have, you've come all the way down from
Scotland, haven't you? Such a shame.'

'Sort of,' said Flora. There was no way she was going to ask
which of the relatives had collected Lorimer's 'bits and pieces'.
There were so many, and any one of them was capable of
pipping her at the post in the biography stakes, given half a
chance. Poor old Looney. She knew his funeral would not
make the local news, and that Mrs Endersby knew it too and
despised them all accordingly. She hadn't even let him smoke,
poor old bugger, probably not even an exploding cigar for old
times' sake.

'He wouldn't want you to upset yourself', said Mrs Endersby.
'Dear old Looney, we'll miss him. He was always such a merry
soul, never complained. Are you in the Profession yourself? No,
I thought not. Never mind, I'm sure our Looney's got them all
in fits up in Heaven now!'

'I bet you say that to all the girls,' Flora muttered as
Mrs Endersby cocked an ear ceilingwards as if to catch the
gales of angelic laughter. All Flora could hear was, 'If you don't
want the whelks, don't muck 'em abaht.'

'Doesn't that man ever sing anything else?' she asked, taking
a tissue from a conveniently sited box.

'Oh, that's our Corky. Quite a card is our Corky. Keeps us
on our toes, bless him,' she added grimly. 'Oh, I almost forgot.
Mr Loney left something for you. He was most particular you
should have it. I'll just ask Mrs Ho to fetch it before you go.'

She left the door open as she went into the hall and shook
the little bell. Flora heard an exasperated female voice say, 'Put
it away now, Chippy. It's not clever and it's not funny.'

Flora's heart was beating faster. Great Uncle Lorimer had
thought of her at the last. If only she hadn't put off the
visit. Mrs Endersby returned, followed by the sex-slave, now
identified as Mrs Ho, carrying a white cardboard box. Flora
took it awkwardly.

'Aren't you going to open it?' asked Mrs Endersby.

'See what your uncle give you,' Mrs Ho encouraged.

84   Flora hesitated. Mrs Ho was probably very keen on ancestors and would think that Flora was dishonouring Great-Uncle Lorimer by her lack of enthusiasm, but she was afraid to open the box. It was as if she might find Great-Uncle Lorimer inside, shrunk to the size of a doll or a mummified monkey in a clown's costume. She prised up a corner, then lifted the lid. On a bed of faded pink tissue paper lay a pair of clown's shoes.

Cradling the box like a baby she hadn't wanted, Flora said, 'I wonder why . . .'

A younger woman, in pale blue, hurried in, saying, 'Sorry to butt in, but could you come please, Mrs Endersby? There's been an Incident in the Big Top!'

Flora followed them into the hall and saw, through a half-open door at the end of the corridor, old men in dressing gowns on a circle of chairs under the bright circus mural running round the walls. Mrs Endersby, excusing herself, strode towards the Big Top. Mrs Ho showed Flora out.

As she sat in the car, hoping that her orange carnations, which she had left on the sofa in the Visitors' Lounge, would perk up in water and give pleasure to the poor souls in the Big Top, but suspecting that they would find a home in Mrs Endersby's sanctum, a minicab drew up beside her, and as it reversed, Flora glimpsed a white masklike face at the passenger window. She pulled away quickly. So it had been Great-Uncle Lorimer's room that they were hoovering. She remembered a children's television programme which had shown how clowns register their make up by painting it on an egg, which was then stored in the vault of a special clowns' church in the East End of London. What was the copyright on a greasepaint smile, Flora wondered, ten years, fifty years, a hundred years, eternity? Or would, somewhere in the East End tonight, an eggshell be smashed?

'Oh no, not clown shoes! I must be in for some pretty bad news!' Flora's mother, Janet, said, when Flora telephoned her that evening.

'What do you mean, Mother? I've just *given* you some pretty bad news.'

'It's a song. "Clown Shoes." I've been trying to remember all the words for years, and who it was by. Was it Johnny Burnett? Anyway, darling, of course it's sad about Lorimer, but he had a good innings, or whatever clowns have, and I hardly knew him. He *was* your father's uncle, you know. Anyway, in the song, this girl sends her boyfriend a pair of clown shoes as a way of telling him they're through. It's hilarious – as if sending clown shoes were standard teen-jilting protocol. Do you think there was a special clown shoe department in the shoe store, or that they had to get them from a circus? Anyway, it ends up with the boy putting the clown shoes on. Sad. Can't you just see the High School Hop, with all the Jilted Johns bopping around in clown shoes?'

'No, mother. I'd better ring Daddy.'

'Poor Looney. I wonder what they did with his wig. It was green. Looney was a punk before his time. I wonder if that's where Keith got it from.'

'Of course he didn't.'

One of Flora's cousins had enjoyed brief local fame, in Maybole, as Keith Grief, lead singer with the Kieftans.

Flora, lying on her sofabed, with a packet of Marks and Spencer's cream cheese and chive crisps to hand, Mozart's Requiem playing quietly, dialled Aberdeen, picturing her father in a claret-coloured corduroy jacket which, in fact, his third wife had thrown out years before. He was on his fourth marriage now. Flora was the child of his second. When Flora had been a little girl, she had wanted to be a poet in a jacket with leather elbow patches. She had had her own study in the kneehole of Daddy's desk, where she had written her poems on a toy typewriter, but Daddy had left when she was five and her brother Hamish was three. Flora's latest stepmother, Isobel, picked up the phone.

'Hello, Flora, how are you? Have you got snow down there too? What's the weather like?'

'Dreich,' said Flora. 'Foggy. A real mushroomsouper.'

'You'll be wanting a word with your father. Hang on, I'll give him a shout. He's just sorting out the boys' computers.'
'Don't bother,' Flora almost said, bitterly, but remembering that she was the bearer of bad news, forbore to hang up.

Isobel had taken to calling herself Bel lately. Wedding photographs showed long brown hair cut in a fringe, under an Alice band of ice-blue roses, huge hazel eyes swimming behind hexagonal spectacles, dangling earrings, a gift from the groom, an outfit with too many lapels and a blue carnation in silver paper and a brooch, a blouse with gilt-trimmed buttons the size of quails' eggs. The Mail Order Bride, Janet called her. With all his faults, nobody could deny that George, 'Dod', Loney was a worker, a grafter. That was what they said of him. He was a fanatical supporter of his football team, the Dons, and he had dreamed once of captaining Scotland in the Poetic League, so to speak. Now, here he is, turning out in all weathers for third-division fixtures, stiff-legged in his impeccable old-fashioned kit, bringing a whiff of brilliantine, starch and dubbin to the field of younger players, and the price-tag of all those goalless draws, lost matches and substitutions could be read in the lines of his face. As if the fouls and penalties of literary life were not enough to contend with, Dod had a young wife who had published her own first slim volume of verse about childbirth, *Drupes and Pomes*, a son who was making a name in the book pages of the English papers, and a daughter who was threatening to write a biography of a talent greater than himself, a profligate who had squandered his gifts, scored over and over again with an effortless arc of the ball from an impossible angle, and who had been stretchered off in disgrace before half-time. Dod sucked on a bitter wedge of lemon.

Flora heard his feet on creaking stairs, loping up from the basement den, thought of her tin typewriter, and hardened her heart against his craggy charm and iron-blue hair.

'Fit like, Flora?'

'I'm well, thank you Father. But the bearer of bad news, I'm afraid.'

'I've heard.'

'Oh. It was surreal, I went there, to Grimaldi House, and it was full of ancient clowns. Great-Uncle Lorimer had left me something, you'll never guess . . .'

From his study window Dod could see the statue of Wallace in Union Terrace Gardens with a bonnet of snow. He interrupted Flora.

'Ah well, he had a good – clownings. I suppose that puts paid to your notion of attempting the Life, then?'

'On the contrary, Father. They're getting a baby elephant to pull the hearse, as a mark of respect.'

ROBIN ROBERTSON

VISITING MY GRANDFATHER

In a room as dark as his
you remembered colour, in amongst
brown bakelite, teak,
and felt for furnishing,
the black-out curtains from the war.
I saw the blue cuneiform of the crossword
looming under the magnifier
for my father to finish;
the slow valves of the radio
warming like coals
into English voices;
the rainbow spills, for his pipe,
in a beaker by the hearth.
And the fire, of course, when lit,
full of all the usual pictures:
caves, dragons, life.
But being children
we were out too far to feel the heat,
kicking our legs on the high chairs,
nursing our flat lemonade
and trying not to see our blurred ghosts
in the dresser's unsilvering glass.

Once a year, though, it was summer,
and in the great window

were the white yachts of Stonehaven,
the yellow yachts in the bay.
As if colour TV
had come to Scotland, all afternoon
we watched a testcard
of acid primaries
on wavelengths of green
and a lemony blue.

It was a chill parlour, despite the fire,
but leaving was like opening
the door of a fridge: cold
dumping on your sandalled feet,
your bare legs.
Finding my way back from the kitchen,
arms out in the dark
for the connecting door,
I came against
a womanly thing,
some kind of shawl
or handbag dressed in feathers,
which I felt all over,
putting my hands down below—
till I touched the wetness,
neck and sudden beak,
left it swinging as I ran,
leaving half my life behind
with the hung pheasant
and half in my hands with its blood:
cinnabar, carnelian,
rose madder, rust.

90

THE IMMORALIST

In the sleeping ward, night-nurses
gather at my curtained bed,
looming like Rembrandts, drawing
their winged heads in around
the surgeon at my side.
The golden section lit by anglepoise:
the wrinkled fruit, some books,
my chest strapped like a girl's
to stem the leaking wound.

Scissoring the grey crêpe
released a clot dark as liver:
an African plum in its syrup
slid into my lap.
Jesus, I said, as the doctor called for swabs,
more light, the stitching trolley.
Without anaesthetics he worked quickly,
his pale hands deft
as a guitarist at the frets.
This is what they'd been waiting for:
one hand at the pliant flesh,
the other subduing it with suture
and a blurred knot.
Five minutes and it was over,
and he was smiling at the Gide
amongst the magazines and grapes:
Used to be just TB, this place, he said,
my blood on his cheek like a blush.

As the nurse drew back the curtain, she warned:
There will be pain.
Night flooded, streaming slowly into shape;
I heard the tinnitus of radio,
saw the humped figure under his lung of light,
the earphones' plastic stirrup on its hook,

his left hand in place on the white bandage
his right hand holding my book.

THE FLOWERS OF THE FOREST

Shouldering my daughter
like a set of pipes
I walk her
to a dead march
and counterpoint her crying
with my hummed drone:
the floo'ers o' the forest
are a' wi'ed awae

my cracked reed
blanking
on the high note,
the way a nib runs dry
in the rut it makes,
and splays.

SILVER LAKE, VERMONT

Familiar gestures in a fresh hand:
the lint and balsam,
sanctuary of the cooled flesh.
Under a tissue moon, your hair untied,
your hair held back, the balm
of chrism dribbed against your side.

A THEORY OF LITERARY CRITICISM

By Douglas Dunn

In 1930, on the island of Java,
Pablo Neruda purchased Shakespeare's *Sonnets*
Into which he wrote his name and the date.

After he died, his houses were plundered.
What became of his book, his treasure of four decades?
Whether stolen, or cast aside, it circulates

From Batavia to Chile by the long way round
Across the Indian Ocean and the South Atlantic,
From Chile to Batavia across the Pacific.

It goes like an albatross and they cannot kill it.
Out of the fires of burning books rises the perfect replica.
From hand to phantasmagorical hand

It visits 'the perfume of pomegranates in Verona',
'The vulgar voices of parasites and buffoons',
And touches men and women to the quicks of their lives.

Burning purifies it. They cannot kill it.
It runs off the printing presses; and they cannot
    kill it.
They discuss it in lecture theatres but cannot kill it.

Were it sought out by police everywhere, and none
    remained,
Keepers of verse would whisper it to others
And teach them with memory's astounding patience.

They would write it down for them, in every language.   93
Anything made can be unmade, but with this exception . . .
If it exists, it exists, and there is the chance of eternity.

SEVEN POEMS

By Tom Leonard

Proem

who are we, trapped in our ways
                 of dying towards the fact
of only once having been, together

or separate in our own being
         but never wholly separate, only a part
of the time we live in, and with others occupy

(1)

your eyes

the iris grey or is it green
the blue iris

we both love
safely, using the word

and the freschia
with the smell of freschia

filling the room
coming home,
surprised

that place we share

(2)

who wants to be free
who has need of air

who is changing

who has a different definition
who has no definition

instance
(the right)

who wants to find out what it is
who wants to go forward

who wants to

From *The Institution*,
(a work in progress)

Skills

inventing jobs
teaching the skills

of applying for jobs

–

one of millions
training

to acquire the skills
to apply for jobs

–

not out of a job
but training

to apply for a job
and to be in a job

efficiently

–

co-operating with management
competing with colleagues

learning the ropes

–

96 ## Firmly

It would be wrong not to say
this is what happened. But

considering all other points of view
as not totally invalid in themselves;

it might be safer to say nothing
about the whole incident, and

rest assured that whatever you or I
may think of it, the matter is closed.

Opting for early retirement

time only/
time management

reified agency
of cost-function conscience

numerical value
constantly

defining the scope
of being-in-the-structure

taboo being
unpredictable being

being as quantum
being as inefficient

motor tasks
establishing targets

recognising actual deficiencies
establishing potential deficiencies

guilty until innocent
the human as an agent of deficiency

the question always
and the answer always

surely total innocence is impossible

The underfunders' utopia

the state hospital
with one bed

always full
always efficient

PROPOSAL

By Janice Galloway

Shit
   zeroed through two walls and into her ear, bloomed there like a bomb.

The way his voice could do that, just find her out: through precast concrete and pebbledash like a heat-seeking missile, just straight through solid structures. The windows not even open.

   Shit
   coming closer.

Then the door sprung off its catch and a blur of what had to be Callum shot by the back of the settee. She knew it had to be Callum because of the way the air displaced, shifting out his road. Also he spoke. It's only me jesus crying out loud there's birdshit all over the fucking car for godsake, he said. And door slammed back again, him outside, her in. The reverberation of his voice hung on, though. Palpable. Irene imagined if she sat very still, screwing her eyes up, she'd be able to see it: wee lines radiating from the space he had occupied then abandoned, like in a cartoon. She kept sitting, waiting till whatever the lines were made of melted then got off the settee. It was ok. It was always ok. Just Callum, that excitable way he got – in the cupboard and out of it before you even had time to turn round. He would be outside with his polishing cloth again, quite the thing. She imagined him scouring, lifting the rag with wee daisies he'd made out of an old sheet. He'd lift it up and glare

at the wee daisies for not trying hard enough, then press them
back down hard, scouring till the windows gave in. Spotless,
like they weren't really there. The way he liked them.

Irene? Five minutes ok?

A dunt at the door, feet on gravel, car locks freeing and
slamming. He'd have a heart attack before he was thirty at
this rate. She was never done telling him and he was never
done kidding on he couldn't hear. Irene couldn't blame him.
Nagging, you called it: what husbands gave in evidence they
were Not Understood when they spoke to strange women in
pubs, what they couldn't talk to other men about for fear they
be thought less of. She lifted the empty glass on the coffee
table, looked into it. If she didn't take it through, rinse it
now, there would be a ring of dried-out sherry welded onto
the bottom when they got back. Everything else was done:
cases out, sockets switched off, doors pulled over, the curtain
arranged so it looked not shut and not open at the same time.
She glanced across at the kitchen, back down at the glass, then
raised it, tilting her head back for a last drop that didn't come.
What did was a clear picture of the corner of the ceiling.
Those marks up there. They were definitely getting worse.
Not just dots and maybe-not-there-at-all things but noticeable
greynesses, widening out. A piece of wallpaper was lifting from
the border as well, something blurry, fungal maybe, creeping
out from underneath.

Irene? Cmon. It's now or never.

She put the glass down on the mantelpiece, reached for her
bag, draped the strap over one shoulder without taking her eyes
off the ceiling. The car horn sounded. Twice. Irene bounced
the keys in her hand, still looking up. Then turned her heel
quickly and opened the door.

Callum wasn't in the car. He was staring at the guttering and
pointing.

Look at that, he said, Look.

The gutter was glutted with chicken bones.

Bloody dogs at the bin bags again, he said. You think folk would feed their own mutts. Look at it. Terrible. He rubbed his hands together and looked up then, smiling. We ready for the off?

Irene looked at him.

We got everything?

Callum, she said. She hoped it sounded irritating.

He looked back, blank. Not playing.

How come knowing whether we've got everything is my area of expertise, exactly? Why's it my responsibility?

His eyebrows had sunk. He hadn't a clue what the matter was. Irene tilted her head to one side, sighing. There was no point forcing it.

Yes, she said. Yes. We've got everything.

He went back to the smiling, the mild abrasion of his palms. Irene poked her arse and one foot inside the car, keeping her knees as together as possible. The dress rode over her thighs anyway, a pale triangle of knicker showing through the crotch of her tights when she sat down but she said nothing. It was one thing being fed-up with the weeness of the MG but another being sarky about it. He was quite right: the so-called witticisms about sports cars and penile length were no longer funny. Besides, the frock wasn't his fault. He might well have suggested she wear the damn thing, said if he had the choice he would wear a dress now and again, but it was her that had put it on. Anyway, dresses were better for you. They didn't give you thrush and compression marks the way jeans did. He was right about that as well.

Hey look, he was saying. He was pointing at the floor. New rugs.

She saw things like red toilet seat surrounds, black letters chasing themselves under her feet. HERS. HERS HERS HERS HERS HERS in an endless loop. Callum's had their own railtrack. HIS HIS HIS HIS HIS.

Two for the price of one, he said. He was turning the ignition and looking over, thrilled to hell. Good, eh?

He stroked her leg, laughing, his mouth wide open. Irene couldn't think the last time she'd seen him in this kind of mood. Laddish. Like a wee boy. It was more than the new rugs, more than the daftness he'd bought them for. He looked over at her then, his eyes shiny: a look that said she was a thing of beauty, a joy forever. It was the frock. It didn't matter how crabbit she was being, he was loving seeing her in the bloody thing. They were going on holiday and she was wearing a frock. Irene looked at the smile, at Callum behind it.

There's paper coming off the wall in the livingroom, she said. That bit near the skylight. I told you it needed redecorating.

He shook his head in a manner suggestive of astonishment, one side of the smile widening.

I don't know, he said. You're unreal, you. He shook his head again, good-natured, flicked the indicator switch. He laughed out loud. You're un-bloody-real.

Callum's mum was in the kitchen surrounded by smells of spitting meat. Callum ducked to avoid a mobile that hadn't been there before. Lavender bags strung on garden twine, tiny pink bows all down its length.

You've arrived, she said.

No lipstick yet but her nails freshly varnished, pearl-white hearts. Their tips cramped what was left of a cabbage tight against the chopping board, pale green shreds falling in layers to cover the design of little girls in mob caps. She gazed down at the cabbage like the Virgin Mary, keeping slicing. Callum picked a single sliver off the board and held it near his mouth. He always took something when he came in, posed with it till she gave him a mock slap on the wrist so he could so his look of mock outrage. It was a routine. Irene watched them do the whole thing.

When's the dinner ready then? he said. I'm starving.

O you, she said, O you, and rolled her eyes.

There was a recipe for rack of lamb on the pinboard, a corner of an advert still attached. The advert had a woman in corsets,

102   fifties style, her breasts cones. The cardboard horseshoe with a sprig of heather stuck was coming loose. Cousin Angela's wedding favour. Her eldest must be six by this time, Irene thought. Six at least.

Is he not terrible? Mrs Hamilton said.

Irene asked if there was anything she could do, anything needing doing. She meant for lunch but supposed they knew. Mrs Hamilton said she'd give her a shout. It was what she always said. When the shout came, it would be to come and get a basket of bread that was already sliced and carry it through. It was all a shout ever meant. She always asked though. Through the connecting door, the tv was running Tom and Jerry. The news would be next. She watched it till the tune started but didn't go through. Callum never liked her doing that. He liked her to stay with them in the kitchen even if there was nothing she was useful for. He was anxious about it now, looking over while pretending to rummage in the cutlery drawer, exclamation marks showing between his eyes. Irene nodded to let him know it was ok. He poked his thumb into the air to show her he was pleased and went back to the rummaging while Mrs Hamilton lifted their jackets, carried them out to the hall cupboard. The soft sound of receding fur mules, Callum crashing out cutlery in fours.

Two geraniums on the sill: no withered leaves, no fallen blooms. Beyond them, Irene saw Callum's father working, making holes in the dark garden border soil. His hair had been cut, the temples shot with more grey. She watched him reach and ferret forth something from a plastic bag, something with roots that would fit the hollow he had just cleared with his bare hands. Dirty but fine boned, the wrists narrow. They had worked for a Security firm for twenty-four years, those hands, gloved in leather: the rest of him swathed in navy, a helmet with a full-face visor. Irene watched him work, forcing his fingers into the soil and wondered if he'd ever battered the hell out of somebody during those twenty-four years; gone queerbashing or studied the reader's wives or Dutch porn the other boys kept stashed under the seats of the van. It was entirely possible. He wouldn't have enjoyed it or anything but it was still entirely possible. At that moment, he looked round for something, failed to see it. He stood up instead, wiping his hands along the seams of the trousers he wore for the garden and would wear to the table too. On the edge of the lawn, she could see a pair of garden gloves, the plastic tie unbroken. The ones she had given him for Christmas. To George xxx. Untouched. He strode over them, careful of plant shoots, heading for the house.

The door opened. Mr Hamilton stood on the top step of his own back door, knocking mud off his boots, a loose lock of hair falling forward over his brow as his feet struck the stone. He nodded to Irene, inscrutable. Callum came back through from the livingroom and opened the fridge door.

Aye aye. He spoke to the freezer compartment.

Aye aye. His father nodded again, eyes focussed in the general direction of Callum's feet. All right, then?

Callum looked above the white door rim for a moment, a kind of confused smile coming with him. His face was pink.

Aye fine, he said, the smile stuck. Like he'd been caught doing something naughty. The eyes of the two men met by mistake for a moment before Mrs Hamilton opened the serving hatch. The peach-coloured lipstick she was so fond of, the one that made her mouth look like it had been squeezed out of an icing bag, moved.

You've a clock in that stomach of yours, it said. ESP or something.

George bashed his foot one last time for luck and closed the back door. What is it then? he said. He didn't look at her.

I don't care what it is. Callum looked better suddenly, relieved. Just get it on the table.

Mrs Hamilton looked at them. She looked at Irene. I don't know, she said. Her face plump with happiness, delight even. The things you've to put up with in this house.

104   Mr Hamilton smoothed his hair back, turned away to the sink. He started washing his hands.

It was cabbage, potatoes, cauliflower and carrots. The basket of bread went in the middle: the big plate of roast something, last. The roast always sat next to George because George always carved it. It was George's job. He cut the meat and put it onto plates. Irene's was always first. She took her plate, told him it was fine. Callum took his, looked down at the meat and said, We're going to Belfast.

Silence. Irene looked. She knew from the way the words were hanging over the dinner. The bugger hadn't told them. He'd said he would and he hadn't. It was the first he was telling them now. Mrs Hamilton looked at George, looked away again, held a big spoon of carrots out for general inspection.

Your daddy grew these. What do you think?

Very nice, Callum said. Lovely.

Irene wondered when the fork would come over. Callum usually pinched her meat and gave her his vegetables. He did it particularly when he was trying to be charming. The fork didn't come though. She heard George put down his knife, the silence stiffen up.

When? He said it very slowly. When's this then?

Callum kept his eyes on the salt shaker, poking it as if the holes were blocked. He shoogled it a couple of times.

Soon, he said.

Oh yes. You're going to Belfast, then. Soon.

Callum put the shaker down. Mrs Hamilton settled back.

Everybody got everything they want?

When's that then, George said. Soon? What's that supposed to mean? What for?

Soon. Irene knew from the way he said it he was looking at her, wanting her to look back. Soon, ok? Soon.

He chewed something as though it was burning his mouth, swallowed.

Soon, he said. Tomorrow.

George looked straight at Callum then back at his plate. His
mother doled out cabbage.

For goodness' sake, she said.

Callum ran his finger along the blunt edge of the knife, back
again. He didn't look at her.

You never tell us nothing, she said. It's terrible. Is it a holiday
or what? It's terrible.

George made a noise like clearing cattarh and swallowed.

You could have stayed at your auntie Pat's if you'd let
us know. I don't suppose you've contacted her either. Eh?
Contacted Pat?

Not yet.

Ha. There was a note of genuine pleasure in George's voice,
triumph or something. Irene heard it. Not yet he says ha. I
didn't think so. Not yet eh? Ha!

His knife scraped against the white ceramic.

Stupid, spending money. You could have stayed at Pat's.
Dunno what's wrong with you, boy. Got secrecy like a
disease. He sniffed. I'm taking it on trust you know what
you're doing, boy.

Callum.

His mother's eyebrows had collapsed like a swing bridge. Not
holding bowls or spoons any more, she looked bereft, lonely.
Even her back slumped.

Honest, it's terrible. If you're away on holiday you could just
say. I don't know what you're like that for, son. She looked like
somebody had punched her.

You'll miss the big meeting as well, George said. He mumbled.
You won't be here.

Not even saying, though. She looked at her husband. He was
cutting a potato. You'd think we were bad to him or something.
You'd think we were – then she couldn't think what else they
might be and stopped. Irene looked at Mrs Hamilton, the way
she tried to meet the gaze of people who would not look back.
For six years she had been calling her Mrs Hamilton. Now,
suddenly, she wanted to call her something else.

106   The carrots, she said.

Callum turned. They all did.

These carrots here. They're very nice. Wilma.

Everyone had stopped eating, nonplussed. Then George's face melted.

Course they are, he said. Grew them out there. Organic what-you-call-it. Organic methods. Good for you.

His teeth, clean marble slates, showed briefly. He'd never had a filling in his life. Wilma held out the blue dish still half-full of orange discs.

Here. Her voice was full of something. Have some more, she said. There's plenty.

Belfast, George said. I don't know. But it was better somehow. It was definitely better. Callum raised his eyebrows so only Irene could see, keeping his head down while he slipped his fork over and stole the last slice of her meat.

Oh you, his mother said. Under the peach-coloured smile, the real colour of her lips beginning to show. Oh you.

There was the eating of pudding, the clearing away, the settling of dishes in the sink.

No don't you do them, she said. Away you two through and watch tv.

Singing came through the hatch with the water noises, wee bits of ABBA and godknew. George went to get his roses done before the sky clouded over. Irene and Callum had two cups of tea, a Hitchcock remake and Songs of Praise. The usual Sunday afternoon.

George missed the chips and cold meat and Callum doing the washing up. Callum went out to the shed to fetch him in when they were leaving. They all stood on the front door step except Irene. There wasn't room for four. Mother and son kissed, she on her toes, fingers tipping his shoulders as if she might keel over reaching so high. Father and son didn't. They didn't touch at all. George came down the step for Irene though. He leaned

forward, brushed her cheek with his mouth pursed. Should
wear a frock more often, he said. Nice. Then he stood back
and smiled. He had a beautiful smile, George. They both had
beautiful smiles. Callum looked like both of them whether he
smiled or not. You could see it without even trying.

You taking that thing? George pointed at the car. You serviced
it then?

Callum got in, rolled the window down. It's fine, dad.

Fine for a heap of junk. Bet it won't start first time.

It did. Callum stuck his head out the window, triumphant.
His father smiled again: unstinting, clean. He waved.

See and have a nice time, Wilma shouted. She waved too.
George and Wilma smiling on the front porch, forearms ticking
like metronomes. They kept doing it till the car was out of sight.
Callum relaxed into the driving seat, changed gear.

Heap of junk, he said. Cheeky bastard.

Three EXPECT DELAYS signs were evenly spaced along the
approach to the shore road. The shore road was usually ok.
Sunday nights it was hardly ever busy at all. Tonight it was a
risk. Callum took it anyway. He weighed the possibilities and
made a decision. After ten minutes or so with no trouble, he
relaxed. Irene didn't realise till he did it he'd been anything
else. He put his hand on her leg, patting it lightly.

Ok?

Irene said nothing.

The patting became a long stroke, knee to thigh, back down
to rest where it started.

What time we due at your mother's then?

Ten.

She knows we're coming?

Of course she knows. I told her not to make up the spare
room. Told her we'd do it.

Callum's hand cut off at the wrist by the black jersey, white
against the orange tights. Irene stared at it.

108   Callum, she said. She paused, choosing the right words, the moment. How come you never said to your folks about us going away? The hand moved back to the steering wheel. He looked in the rear-view mirror, back out front again, checking something. He checked it for ages.

Callum I'm asking you a question.

I did tell them. They must have forgot.

Irene levelled her eyes on his face. Callum. You didn't tell them.

I did.

No you didn't.

I did.

Irene sighed. Callum blushed right down to his neck.

I did. They must have forgot. Honest.

Callum. She bent his name into a hillock. He looked at her out the corner of an eye and sighed.

Ok ok, he said. Ok so I didn't tell them. I own up it's a fair cop guv I'll never do it again. Satisfied?

No I'm not satisfied. I know perfectly well you didn't tell them. I don't want to know *whether*, Callum. I want to know *why*. *Why* didn't you tell them?

He drove, staring hard at the road. His chin disappeared.

I just didn't want any hassle.

What hassle?

The twenty questions thing. You know what he's like about the car, telling me what I should be doing and all that stuff. You know what he's like, Irene.

You could have told your mother. Her voice was down to its usual octave again, coaxing. Cmon. You could have said to her on the phone.

He sighed again.

There was nothing stopping you.

What difference does it make eh? It's ok now. They weren't bothered.

They were so bothered. More to the point I was bothered. Me, Callum. *I* was bothered.

Aw cmon Irene.

Cmon nothing. I *was*. They must think I'm a rude bastard, that I was in on it or something.

In on it? In on what for godsake? I'm twenty-two for christsake Irene: I don't need to tell my father everything I bloody do. Am I supposed to be asking for permission or something, is that it?

That's a complete side-issue, Callum, *completely* beside-the-point. The point is not about asking permission: the point is you told me you DID and you bloody *hadn't*. You *hadn't*.

So?

So you gave me misinformation. You made me look like an idiot and/or an accomplice and I don't like it.

Oh for fucksake Irene.

Don't fucksake me, Callum. You did. Either they thought I was in on not telling them, on not giving a toss what they thought *or* they've picked up the fact you never tell me what's going on half the time either. I don't like it. I don't like not being told what's going on. It's embarrassing.

Callum snorted.

It is. It's humiliating. I don't like being shown up in front of folk like that. Especially not your parents. It's controlling and humiliating and I feel belittled by it.

Belittled. He said it like it was a foreign word. Belittled?

The car was slowing down, tacking behind a queue of others. Yellow lights were flashing up ahead somewhere. Callum pulled up the handbrake. The creaking died away.

That's ridiculous, Irene. That's the most ridiculous thing I ever heard.

No it isn't.

Yes. It. Is.

Irene turned to the side window. Outside was getting dark now, the sea washing with nothing to glitter off. She watched it come and go in the half-light, mist gathering in the corners of the window.

I don't know why you're doing this.

It was a very measured voice. She turned round. Callum was

110 shaking his head, holding the wheel with both hands. The car was rolling, almost imperceptibly.

Oh for godsake. She sighed. Are we going to play a you–started–it game?

Silence. Big silence.

Look. Irene breathed heavily down her nose, rubbed her temples hard. Ok. I'm doing this badly. What I'm really trying to say is you don't need to be so . . . whatever it is.

I don't need to be so what?

Manipulative, Callum. That's what you don't need to be. Telling lies about trivial wee things then getting annoyed when I find out. Like I'm not supposed to let on I've noticed.

He pulled the brake back on full, his mouth set.

Me. *I* tell *you* lies? I tell you *lies*?

Ok maybe it's not lies. Evasions then. Is that a less contentious word–choice?

He said nothing for a moment, just glared at the windscreen. Sometimes. He said it like the first number in a countdown. Sometimes, Irene, you can be a sarcastic cow.

That's as may be, she said. But you're still doing it. You're avoiding the issue, steering the conversation away from what I'm trying to say.

Which is?

Which is – her voice was getting louder again, hard to keep control of – which is, Callum, you telling me you'd told your folks when you hadn't. The issue is you controlling information and not telling the truth.

I do tell you the truth.

You tell me the truth?

Yes. I do.

Ok. You tell me the truth, then. Tell me it now. I'd like the truth about this meeting, please.

What meeting?

This meeting you won't be there for. Tell me about that.

Callum said nothing.

That's all I know, there's some meeting and you won't be

there – and I only know *that* because your dad said, only there was other stuff going on at the time. Now there isn't so you can tell me. What meeting? On you go.

I don't know. I don't know what he was talking about.

Irene looked at him. She kept looking at him. Callum intensified his gaze on the nothing that was behind the windscreen.

Are you being serious? she said.

Eh? He screwed his face up as though something was annoying him, as though he was concentrating really hard and not able to hear her. Eh?

I said—

Callum sounded the horn suddenly, leaning hard on the middle of the steering wheel.

Look at this carry on, he said. Look. Bloody road works eh?

Irene turned away. She banged her head off the side window. Then she did it again. I give up, she said. She exhaled very slowly. I. Give. Up.

Her hair had brushed a gap in the condensation. Through the streaky mesh, she could see the shore wall still there, the mission rock behind it. ETERNITY. She could see it quite clearly: the paint luminous at this time of night. Nothing else, not even the sea. Just the rock and its message, a present from the holy rollers who prowled the seafront with a bucket of whitewash every summer. They had cookouts and things, sang hymns. ETERNITY. Irene looked at the letters, the gaps between them. She was wondering how often they did it, repainting the same thing to keep it clear, whether they came at night to keep the whole thing a kind of mystery. Maybe you were meant to think god had done it, or something. Then it clicked. George saying All right? that way, Callum going coy. The conversations she'd heard father and son having umpteen times and thought were just one-sided. It clicked.

112   You've joined the Lodge, haven't you? she said. You've joined the bloody Orange Lodge.

She turned and looked at him. He was looking back at her, his face flushed.

No wonder you're fucking embarrassed. She was staring at him so hard her eyes hurt. Christ on wheels Callum. The Orange Lodge.

Callum's mouth was open but nothing was coming out. He looked caught. Scared. Ridiculous. For no reason, without seeming to want to, Irene started laughing. A steady through the nose snort. Callum looked away quickly, crunching into the wrong gear, back out again. The car in front had started moving. Callum let the motor inch forward, closing the gap carefully but the engine was revving. Irene didn't drive but she knew it didn't need to rev that hard. The laugh had died away now, stopped as fast as it had come. A string of red lights flashed on down the whole slope of the hill. The car settled on its hunkers again, rocking slightly.

He was still saying nothing, just sniffing. After a moment he made little coughing sounds, sniffing some more.

Jesus christ almighty, she said. She didn't turn round, just kept staring down. The pattern on the frock rose and fell with her breathing, rose and fell. She watched it, waiting. Then looked up. His eyes were very shiny, trained on the tail-lights ahead.

Dad put my name up, he said. I thought I could do something he'd like for a change. That's all. Doesn't matter.

He rubbed the bridge of his nose, wiped one side of his face with the back of his hand. The other held on to the steering wheel. It held on tight. The insides of the windows were steaming up again. The car was completely still.

What are we doing, Irene?

His voice was so soft, she hoped for a moment he hadn't spoken at all. He had though. She said nothing waiting.

Everything, he said. Everything is up in the air all the fucking time. Can't even visit my parents these days without something, some bloody thing . . .

He ran out of words and leaned forward on the steering
wheel.

Look. I wasn't trying to keep things from you. Honest. I'm
not trying to do anything, just get on with a normal life. That's
all I want. I want us to have a normal life for godsake. You and
me. That's all I'm trying to do.

And all I want is to be let in on things. I want you to stop
making decisions for me.

He sat up again, glared at her.

It's still the engagement ring isn't it?

Irene said nothing.

You just can't let it go, can you?

Irene said nothing.

Ok, he said. I confess, I confess. I did a terrible thing: I bought
you an engagement ring. Yes, I know I should have asked you
first. I know I shouldn't have told anybody we were getting
married before I asked you either. I know I know. I said I was
sorry. Most women would have managed to find something
flattering about it but there you go. I have to say I'm sorry. So
I did. And I am. And I'm still getting this shit.

Irene said nothing.

Jesus christ Irene, what are you wanting me to do though?
I don't go on about what you've done. That affair you had,
that bloody John guy or whatever his name was. I don't keep
dragging that up. I've tried to put it behind me. We need to
put in a bit of effort for christsake, move forward. You don't
fucking try.

Irene said nothing.

What are you thinking?

Nothing.

I know what I think.

Nothing.

I think we should get married.

This time she groaned. He just kept going.

I've asked you often enough. If we got married things would
be different, all sorts of things. You'd see.

114   The engine purring, a stink of damp dog. Looking down, the short blue hem, her legs swathed in orange mesh. Tights. She was wearing tights because. Because. The word HERS HERS HERS coursing under her feet. She could think of nothing to say.

Please. His voice was clear and sure. All you need to do is show willing, Irene. That's all.

He swallowed, didn't look at her.

I don't want us to go off the rails again.

After a while the car in front started to pull away, this time more definitely. Callum reached for the glove compartment, took out the cloth and wiped the inside of the windscreen clear. Irene took it from him, their fingers touching briefly, and finished the rest. It was her job anyway. Slowly, he released the handbrake. Callum's big, competent hands. Like George's. Just like his dad's.

What time did you say we were due at your mother's then? he said.

The side-window showed nothing. Irene rolled it down, watching the glass level fall, breathing deep. Ozone and pitch black. that's all there was. The sea was out there somewhere but only in theory. There was nothing of it visible at all. She had a notion for a moment to ask him to stop, pull the car over so they could go outside, walk for a bit on the sand. But the line was moving. They were inside Callum's car going to her mother's to spend the night ready for the morning ferry. She'd be waiting for them now, watching tv and wondering where they'd got to, nipping in to check the big bed with the top sheet turned back. Everything would be waiting. Irene tucked the cloth away where it belonged, spoke to the windscreen.

I told you already, she said. Ten. She's expecting us at ten.

We're going to be late, he said.

Ahead, the motorway lights, official apologies on reflective metal. Cars picking up speed.

QUESTION NUMBER TEN

By Gordon Legge.

So I goes for this job interview and the boy says, 'Right, name fifty singles by The Fall.'

I goes, '*What?*'

The boy goes, 'You heard me. Come on. Two minutes. Two minutes and counting.'

And I needed it . . . but I did it.

The boy puts a wee tick in this ledger-type book that's lying in front of him.

'Right,' he says, 'next: you know how some folk screw their faces up when they smoke, and how some folk straighten their faces out when they smoke?'

I goes, 'Aye.'

The boy puts a wee tick in his book.

Then he stares us right in the eye. 'Reincarnation,' he says, 'what d'you reckon?'

I shrugs. 'Kind of looks like it to me,' I says.

The boy puts down another tick. Tick number three. Nice wee column of ticks developing.

'Question Number Four,' he says, 'Question Number Four. What d'you do when the adverts are on?'

'Play back the week's goals,' I says.

The boy looks chuffed Another tick goes in the book.

'Four out of four,' he says 'Not bad.'

The boy has a wee laugh to himself.

I has a wee laugh and all. Give him his due, this guy's alright.

'And in summer?' he says.

116   He's caught me off guard. Then it dawns on me – *he's trying to be fly*.

'In summer,' I says, 'I try and get the zero on the video counter using only the rewind and fast forward buttons.'

The boy's into it. He puts down a tick then goes into this wee drawer of his, pulls out a sheet of tracing paper, peels off a wee gold star and sticks it down beside tick number five.

'Incidentally,' he says, 'much money you got on you?'

'Eh,' I says, digging into my pocket.

'No,' he says, 'I want you to tell me, son. You mean you don't know?'

'Aye,' I says, 'course I do. There's two pound coins, a pound note, a fifty, three twentys, a five and four ones.'

'Well,' he says, 'that's what I was wanting to know, son. Mind: when folk ask you questions, you give them answers, you don't waste their time.'

I nods to the boy. He's got a point. He puts a tick in his book and I breathes a sigh of relief. It was touch and go for a minute there.

'Right,' he says, 'two quickies – when was the last time you told a lie?'

'Bout five year ago,' I says.

The boy puts down a tick.

'And,' he says, 'how long does half a pound of cheese last?'

'Twice,' I says.

The boy puts down a tick.

'You're doing well,' he says, 'doing well. Keep it up. Only two to go.'

I nods to the boy.

'Now tell me,' he says, 'you worked out how you would cheat on *Gladiators*?'

'Aye,' I says . . . but I holds back from telling him. I'm no wanting to waste his time. I'm only telling him what he's wanting to know.

The boy stares us out. I stares him out.

The boy's got this big grin on his face. 'Well done,' he says, 117
'you're learning.'

The boy puts down a tick. He makes a wee note beside it.

'Right,' he says, 'so far, so good. All I'm prepared to say,
son, is that the ball's at your feet. Get my drift?'

I nods to the boy.

'Right,' he says, 'last question. Question Number Ten.'

'I'm listening,' I says.

The boy takes a deep breath. 'Question Number Ten,' he says.
'Question Number Ten – and, by the way, good luck, son.'

I nods to the boy.

'Okay,' he says, 'here we go. Question Number Ten –
would you rather a) be good-looking or b) have a decent-
sized knob?'

I thinks about it.

It's a toughie.

I says, 'Could you repeat the question, please?'

'Certainly,' he says. 'Question Number Ten – would you
rather a) be good-looking or b) have a decent-sized knob?'

I'm all agitated. Jesus, you'd think I'd never thought about
it before.

The boy puts a cross next to Question Number Ten.

He closes his book, puts his pencil down and leans back with
his hands behind his head.

'Sorry, son,' he says, 'time's up.'

He puts the book back in the drawer he got the gold
star out of.

'Now, sir,' he says, 'if you wouldn't mind just leaving your
details with the girl at reception then we'll put you on file and
let you know if any vacancies crop up in the near future. In
the meantime, thank you, that'll be all for now.'

The boy takes a report from the other side of his desk. He
starts skimming through it.

I sits there. I'm no moving.

The boy looks up. He's looking at us like I'm a dafty.

'That'll be all,' he says, 'thank you.'

118   The boy nods towards the door.

I says, 'It's the knob, eh? Eh, it's the knob.'

'I'm sorry, sir. You must understand I can't possibly go into your answers. Now, like I say, if you'd like to just . . .'

I leans over the table. 'No,' I says, 'it's no the knob, though, is it? No, it's no, is it?'

'Good day to you, sir,' he says. 'Now if you would be so kind as to . . .'

I makes a lunge at the boy. I grabs a hold of his lapels and starts shaking him.

'Come on, you,' I says, 'tell me, I want to know, I need to know this.'

As I goes for his throat I notice the boy's looking over to his left.

I looks over to his left and all.

There's a wee green light flashing above his door.

Two seconds later, two guys with short-sleeved blue shirts come bombing in.

And that's the last I mind of it.

THE OPEN UNIVERSITY

Iain Crichton Smith

When Hugh opened the big brown envelope which had fallen on to the mat below the letter-box, he saw that he had been accepted for the Open University. He knew it was a mistake but said to himself after a while, 'Why shouldn't I do it? After all, I am not stupid.' And immediately the world around him which was the world of the village became more real to him, and his life more purposeful. He studied the papers for a while and decided that he would do the Foundation Course.

He never found out exactly how the mistake had occurred, but knew that there was another Hugh MacCallum in the village next to his own and it occurred to him that this was how the error had been made.

Hugh was sixty-five years old and very good at genealogies, derivations of names of places, and the meanings of old words. He had left school at the age of thirteen and had later served in the Merchant Navy: he had seen Australia, New Zealand, and South Africa, among many other countries. Why shouldn't he do the Open University? He was no fool, and after all he might have letters after his name, and that would put a spoke in Alastair's wheel. Alastair thought that Mary Maclachlan was the best Gold Medallist there had ever been, though she was so drunk that she had to be supported on to the stage, but Hugh knew better. Hugh knew that the best medallist who had ever been was Anna MacDougall, who had died with cancer of the throat. But you couldn't tell Alastair anything.

Hugh was a bachelor and so was Alastair. Hugh's mother had died when he was forty-eight years old, and now he lived alone.

120   Alastair too lived alone after his sister had died. Once when she was on the train to Yarmouth to the fishing she had pulled the communication cord out of curiosity, and it was only when the other two girls who were with her had pointed to their foreheads that the little man with the moustache, who had run along to the carriage with a notebook, had been placated.

Hugh decided that he would do the Open University. After all, he had a television set and a radio and plenty of time on his hands.

When he told Alastair about it, Alastair was very angry. He knew at once that this represented a threat to their relationship, and said so. 'Anyway,' he said, his moustache bristling, 'what do you want to go to the university for at your age?'

'I am not going to the university,' said Hugh. 'You do this at home. There are what are called assignments.'

'Assignments? What's that?'

'Compositions,' said Hugh, whose left eye blinked compulsively. He also had a habit of twisting his neck around inside his collar when he was nervous or embarrassed.

'And what will you get at the end of it?'

'I will get a degree,' said Hugh. Already he seemed to be moving away from Alastair and from the village, which was in any case dying. There were hardly any children left, and the buses which had once taken them to school were lying rusting in the fields.

'I see what you are at,' said Alastair.

Hugh didn't say anything to this: he knew that Alastair was angry and that this was his method of getting his own back on him. Maybe, he thought, we shall never discuss genealogies again, and the idea bothered him, for these discussions which had gone on endlessly and inconclusively had passed the time for both of them.

'Think of it, Alastair, we shall soon be dead and I might as well spend my time studying. Don't you want to do it yourself?'

'Not at all,' said Alastair bristling. 'Not at all.'

They were silent for a long while and then Alastair excused

himself and went home. It seemed to Hugh that he was saying goodbye to him forever and he didn't like the feeling. He considered that he was doing something very striking and original by studying for the Open University and maybe cutting himself off from the village. But on the other hand why shouldn't he do it? There was nothing wrong with the quality of his mind. He stared out at the sea which he could see through the window. Its horizon stretched into the distance, blue and infinite.

A strange thing happened to Hugh after a while. He was seeing the people of the village as not really people at all. At first he was puzzled about this but then he realised that it must be something to do with the Open University. Also he seemed to be losing his sense of smell, and one day he ate rancid butter without realising it till a long time afterwards. As well as that, he thought that the mountains that he could see from his bedroom were growing smaller. In the old days he would admire the sunset flaring over the hills, but he no longer did so. It was as if the village was becoming a toy to him and in its place there was building up inside his head another place larger than the village which was inhabited by philosophies, paintings, novels, great cities, open seas. It was as if he had renewed his youth and saw the oceans sparkling as they had been then. Dang it, he thought, this is a fine big world I've got myself into. This is a big sky that I'm seeing.

When he looked at Alastair pottering around his house, he saw him as a little fellow with a blue jersey and a moustache. Alastair, he knew, had a history of high blood pressure in his family: this was because they were all abrupt and irascible. Of course his father had been a bard, like Alastair himself, but what were their poems compared to the ones he was reading now. Childish, that was what they were.

The bees hummed about the moor and when he put his feet down in the spongy moss it was not as it had been. The birds seemed different and so was the sea, and so was the cow which he saw staring at him one day, a long blade of fresh green grass in its mouth.

122   He heard in a roundabout way that the schoolmistress, Miss Gibson, didn't approve of what he was doing. The old sour bitch, he thought, she only has her Primary Teacher's Certificate, she doesn't even have a university degree. He had actually been going to consult her about his English, for his greatest difficulty was not in understanding the material but in setting down his answers in correct sentences. Old bitch, he thought, I won't go and see her; if he ever met her he would casually mention the Renaissance and discover what she knew about it. In any case she was rather mad and would scream at the children and throw chalk at them. Nevertheless, he had great difficulty with his sentence structure and would spend hour after hour struggling to compose a version of his answer that would satisfy an examiner. His light could be seen burning at two o'clock in the morning.

But he could feel a coldness all around him. Who was he to do the Open University? Even when he went to the Post Office to send away his completed assignments, Seordag would hardly speak to him.

'Special delivery,' he would say, and she would look contemptuously at the address. She would purse her lips but would not give him the satisfaction of asking what was in the envelope.

He also missed the human presence of Alastair.

He often felt now that he was entirely alone, and at nights he would hear the wind moaning in the chimney. Once he had looked at an egg from which a chick was emerging. The shell shook and broke under the vehement restless assault of life and then the chick, bare and skinny, could be seen pushing and struggling. The crown of the shell fell off, the chick pushed, and sometimes it was entangled with the shell and sometimes it seemed to be clear of it. But it thrust and thrust with determined impatience and finally it was out in the open air, an explorer, a small, thin, skinny adventurer that had shed its armour.

He had his first assignment back. It was only a D, but still a bare pass. Dang it, he thought. I must do better than this.

*   *   *

But while he was reading about Constable and studying his paintings he soon forgot the village. How much richer the land in Constable's paintings was, that river smooth and wide, those lush cornfields, and in the background an old mill. He raised his head from his book and wondered why no one had ever painted the village. Think of all those subtle lights that were everywhere, the pearly grey light that you sometimes saw over the sea. No one had ever painted the people who had left on the boats for Canada and Australia and New Zealand, no one had painted the roofless, once-thatched, houses that were to be found all over the village. No one had painted the disused ruined buses which had once carried children to school but which now lay rusting on their sides among the buttercups and the daisies: or even the blue hills which ringed the village and turned purple in the vague evenings.

He scratched the back of his neck as he thought of these things. Then after a while he left his books and went outside and saw Alastair carrying vegetables into the house from his little wind-blown garden. He went over to him and at first Alastair pretended not to know that he was there. His face was red with the effort of bending down. Finally, he couldn't ignore Hugh any longer and stood in front of him with a turnip and a clump of dirty roots dangling from his hand.

'It's a fine day,' said Hugh.

'It's cold enough,' said Alastair.

'Are the turnips good this year?'

'They're not bad. They're not too wet.'

The breeze stirred Alastair's jersey and he seemed somehow to have shrunken. Hugh felt a little panic quivering in his chest, a tiny mouse of fear. At his age he should be thinking about death, attending the church, reading religious books, and not studying the Renaissance, but he didn't feel like confining himself to spirituality. Constable irradiated his mind.

'Have you been composing any poems?' he asked Alastair.

'I have that,' said Alastair, but he didn't want to let Hugh see them.

124 'What are they about?' said Hugh.

'Oh, there's one about . . .but you won't like it, it's in Gaelic,' said Alastair spitefully.

'But why shouldn't I want to see it?' said Hugh. 'I can read Gaelic as well as you.'

Alastair however was stubbornly silent, and then he said grudgingly, 'It's about the sea.'

Alastair couldn't feel himself settled now in Hugh's company. He felt that Hugh was superior to him, that he knew things that he himself didn't; he felt that Hugh had deserted him, was trying to be better than him. What did his poetry matter? In the old days he would have shown his poem to Hugh and listened to his criticisms of it, but now he didn't want to in case Hugh mocked him. No, he wouldn't show Hugh his poem. After all, Hugh had kept his television on when he was visiting him. He had told him that the programme was in connection with an assignment he was doing, but there was nothing more inhospitable than leaving your television on in front of a visitor. Also he missed his conversations about genealogies. And damn him if he would show him his poem.

What is his poem to me anyway, thought Hugh. It's very thin poor stuff. How could one expect good poetry or bardachd from Alastair who had hardly ever left the village in his life. Look at his stringy neck, his jersey, his dungarees. It seemed to him that he had had a poor opinion of Alastair for a long time, but had refused to admit it to himself. Now he was admitting it.

'If you don't want to show it to me,' he said, 'I don't want to see it.'

'That's that then,' said Alastair, 'I'd better be putting the dinner on.' And he went back into the house. As Hugh was returning to his own house, he saw little Colin coming towards him. Colin was the son of a fisherman called Angus Macleod, and his mother was the daughter of Iain MacFarlane from another part of the island.

Colin was wearing a black magician's robe.

'And how are you today, Colin?' Hugh asked him.

Colin stood and looked at him, not speaking, very shy. Finally he said in a burst of words, 'I've got a magic kit.'

'I can see that,' said Hugh, 'and what tricks can you do?'

'I've got a magic coin,' said Colin, in another burst of words. 'Abacadabra,' he shouted, jumping up and down. 'You have to say abacadabra,' he said seriously. 'What hand have I got my coin in?'

'I don't know,' said Hugh, 'I'm not sure that I know that.'

'It's this one, it's this one,' Colin shouted, and held his hand out, showing the coin. Then he was dashing away, shouting, the triumphant magician.

Hugh stood staring after him. At one time he himself must have been like Colin, but he couldn't remember. He could remember very little of his early childhood except that on his first day in school a small woman with grey hair had told him to use some plasticine, which he did. He couldn't even remember how he had learned English, but he must have done so. In the distance he could see Colin jumping up and down spreading out his black wings. How small this village had become, how strange, he felt; maybe it would have been better for him if he had never left the village in the first place.

The village drowsed in time. The houses seemed sunk, each in its own hollow. At night their television sets told the villagers of other countries, of violence, of foreign streets. Why, they had even stopped cutting peat and were now burning coal, though it was very dear: one or two of the houses were all-electric. In winter there was snow and rain. In autumn one felt the nostalgia of the past; the sea was both shield and stimulus and unimaginable depth, a ring around the village, a blue salty ring. There was an air of despair and weariness everywhere. Alastair himself felt the change in his bones and wished that his sister were still alive so that he could torment her. At least Hugh had his Open University. Tears of rage and self-pity filled his eyes.

*   *   *

126   Alastair worked away at his poem, which was called the 'Song of the Open University.'

Bha fear againn anns a' bhaile
a bha aosd is pròiseil,
smaoinich esan air an oilthigh,
chuireadh e air dòigh e.

Nach robh esan cheart cho math ri
fear sam bith na b'òige,
oir 'na mo bheachd'sa 's na mo bharail
chan eil an t-àit' s gu leòr dhomh.'

We had a man in the village
   who was old and proud.
He thought of the university
   and how he would put it right.
Wasn't he as good as anyone
   who was even younger
   for, 'In my opinion and judgment
   this place is not good enough for me.'

Alastair walked up and down his room, listening to the rhymes. He always composed his poem aloud, not on paper, and some time soon he would recite it to some of the villagers. He should be able to make a good poem, for all his ancestors had been fine bards, and many of his poems were already well known, especially the one about the original coming of the electricity to the village. In fact one or two of them had been sung on the wireless and he had strutted about like a peacock after that. But there were a few verses to be added yet.

Imagine the Renaissance, thought Hugh, as he sat down at his oil-clothed table. The sea that stretched outwards into unimaginable distances, the paintings, the cathedrals. The village seemed to be inhabited by Virgin Marys with their holy children. Its colours were marvellous blues and velvet reds and indigos.

Then he read about the Claude glass in the eighteenth century which was designed to convert an ordinary landscape into a formal picture. Imagine that, he thought. Imagine the sky above Constable, so huge, so vast.

Imagine the crazy cornfields of Van Gogh which seemed to echo his thin shrunken whiskers.

All through the night Hugh worked.

And Alastair continued with his poem.

Dh' fhàg e chompanaich a' gearain,
shuidh e aig a leabhrain
or b'e iadsan a chuid arain;
cha robh fiù di-domhnaich

nach robh e ann an solus an dealain
a' sgrìobhadh is a' sgròbadh,
mar chat a tha air tòir air ealain
le peann an àite spògan.

He left his companions to complain,
he sat at his booklets
for they were now his bread.
There wasn't even a Sunday
that he wasn't in the light of the electricity
writing and scraping
like a cat that is in search of science
with a pen instead of claws

Hugh's father had been in fact the very first person to have a car in the village. It was more a van than a car, for in those days he had a butcher's shop, and he travelled through all the villages selling meat. He had been a good businessman, and his shop was a successful one till one night his car had been hit by a bus, and he had been killed outright. Hugh and his mother were left alone, the shop had to be sold, and the memory of the first van faded.

128   However, in his lonely nights, Hugh thought, My father was a
clever man, everyone said that, and I must have inherited his
cleverness. It's not everyone who would be doing what I am
doing at my age. This thought sustained him, as he read and
worked under the light of the electric bulb.

In the village there was an incomer called Stella Simpson who
kept pigs. She had tried to learn Gaelic, but Alastair made
fun of it.

'Do you know,' he had once said to Hugh, 'that woman said
to me, "Is latha math ann" instead of "Tha latha math ann."'

In spite of that, however, she continued to learn Gaelic.

The villagers didn't like her pigs. They were like big pink
submarines in a sea of mud. They were alien beings; in any
case, pigs would eat anything, even each other.

Stella slopped about in yellow wellingtons and tried to learn
how to cook oatcakes and scones. But these were not successful.
When she went to the Post Office, which was also the local shop,
she often wore a long red coat and black glasses. No one could
make out what her age was, but it was considered that she must
be about fifty. Her face was often dead white like a vampire's
and at other times well-rouged.

She was, however, from England: everyone knew that, though
no one had discovered anything about her background. When
she had arrived first she had asked for buttock steak at the
butcher's van instead of rump steak.

In the summertime she sat on the headland, painting the sea.
'I told her once,' said Alastair gleefully, 'that there was a man
who went out fishing one night and a storm blew up, and he
had to shelter in a cave which was full of rats. "How did he
survive?" she asked me. "Well," I said, "he fed them on fish
till the morning came and he escaped."'

One morning Hugh was passing her house, looking askance at
the pigs which wallowed in the sea of mud, pink and obscene and
naked, when she came out in her yellow wellingtons, carrying
a bucket.

'I hear you're doing the Open University,' she said to
Hugh.

'I am that,' said Hugh.

'That's good,' she said. 'I might be able to help you. I have
paintings. And I have some records. I believe you have to study
music as well.'

The pigs attacked the bucket. Her scarf blew in the wind.

'Yes, I have to do music,' said Hugh. 'That's the worst part
of it. You see, I never learned about music.'

What am I doing talking to this woman, he asked himself. In
the old days I wouldn't have. If the villagers see me talking to
her they'll think I'm courting her. On the other hand, he was
beginning to feel lonely, to miss the company of Alastair who
had become inflexible and distant, especially since the night he
had seen pictures of the Virgin Mary in a book Hugh had.

'So you're becoming a Catholic now,' he said contemptuously
to Hugh.

'Not at all, I'm studying,' said Hugh. But Alastair went away,
snorting incredulously.

'I shall come over and bring you some records. Have you a
record player?' Stella asked.

'No.'

'In that case I shall bring my record player as well.'

What an odd-looking woman, thought Hugh. She tries to be
like one of us, but she isn't really. She cannot disguise the fact
that she is an alien. Even her red coat flung a strange radiance on
the landscape. And as for her pigs, who ever saw pigs in a village?
With their horrible snouts and their vivid fleshy nakedness.

By talking to this woman, by allowing her to come to his
house with her records, he felt that he had crossed another
frontier which was taking him further and further away from
Alastair. And yet at the same time the logic was inevitable. It
was true that he didn't know about classical music, and this
woman might teach him or at least give him an insight into it.
His work was not enough, knowledge was also essential.

When Stella arrived at his house under cover of darkness,

130 she was carrying a torch, a record player, and some records. Hugh ushered her into the living-room where a bright fire was burning. He had put away the dishes, and the room was tidy and warm.

'What a nice little place you have,' said Stella, putting down her burden. She took off her coat without asking Hugh to help her. She looked much prettier, her face composed and relaxed, with a certain amount of colour in it. She was wearing a yellow blouse and skirt.

Well, well, said Hugh to himself, well, well. How women can change.

'Your mother's dead?' said Stella, looking at him keenly.

'Yes, I'm on my own here,' said Hugh. 'She died some years ago.'

'I see you have a picture of her on the wall,' said Stella. 'It is her, isn't it?'

'Yes,' said Hugh.

'A strong-looking woman.' said Stella. And indeed his mother did look formidable in her white blouse staring at the camera and not smiling at all.

'I have brought you some Mozart,' said Stella. 'I presume you have a plug?'

'Oh, yes, I have that,' said Hugh awkwardly. Electrical things were not what he was best at. But this woman seemed to have no trouble with them.

The room, which at times appeared austere and cold, had become humanised. He wondered what his mother would have thought of this woman. 'Not for you, Hugh,' she would have said. 'You don't know anything about her. And she might even smoke.'

And sure enough, before sitting down, she did ask for an ashtray, which she laid on the table beside her. It was one which Hugh had brought home from Australia and which showed Sydney Opera House.

Hugh sat down beside the fire and smoked his pipe, first asking permission.

'My late husband smoked,' said Stella, 'when he was well.

He was ill for a long time,' she added. 'Mental trouble. He became very bitter in argument. I find this place very good for me. I needed the rest. He was a very clever scientist and therefore very ingenious at devising torments for me.'

'Oh,' said Hugh.

'You don't want to know about that,' she said, stubbing out her first cigarette. 'And now we will listen to Mozart.'

That night she told him a great deal about classical music and especially about Mozart, whom she idolised. She and her husband, before he became ill, had often gone to concerts in Bath, where in fact she came from. Music was later the only thing that could soothe her husband's savage breast.

As they listened to the music, she would ask him questions. Why had he wanted to do the Open University? Did he do a lot of studying? When had he left school? Had he read a lot?

Of course, he told her, he had always been reading even when he was in the Merchant Navy. He had read Conrad, Stevenson, Melville. She seemed surprised at this.

'Is that right,' she said, staring at him, her cigarette in a long holder. It was as if she was seeing a strange specimen in the village, as alien to her as pigs were to him.

'Mozart is pure intuitive genius.' she told him. 'Better even than Beethoven.' He listened, and as he did so he seemed to hear what she was talking about, but shortly afterwards he was lost again. He had had no training in that kind of music, no previous understanding of it.

'I see I shall have to teach you a great deal,' she said. 'And now perhaps you could give me a cup of tea.'

The request astonished him, and at first he thought her bad-mannered, but then realised that her blunt demand was quite natural for her. In fact, when he showed her the kitchen, she made the tea herself.

'Have you any biscuits or anything?' she asked him.

'I think so,' he said. He found some digestives, and they ate and drank together in front of the bright fire.

He became aware of the steady ticking of the old grandfather

132 clock which he had inherited. He couldn't understand how this woman was here at all, nor why he was entertaining her, nor why he was listening to classical music. It was like a dream.

'I'll tell you why I came to live in this village,' she told him. 'My husband and I were on holiday here years ago. He was interested in bird-watching, you see. And we enjoyed our visit so much that I decided that I would come and stay. Of course the village was healthier then than it is now. I know what people are saying about me. They think I'm odd and that my oatcakes are appalling, which they are. And so is my Gaelic. But these things don't matter.'

She stubbed out her fifth cigarette. Hugh blew leisurely rings from his pipe.

'It's very courageous of you to do the Open University. Very courageous. And in any case if you don't pass you will have learned a great deal.'

Not pass, thought Hugh, and his face reddened. Of course I'll pass. No question about it. I once climbed the crow's nest even though I was trembling with fear. And I'll pass this too.

'What I'll do is leave the record player and the records here,' she told him. 'There's no point in taking them back. At the moment you know nothing about classical music, it's quite obvious.' Her honesty disconcerted Hugh. He wasn't used to it. One was never as direct as this in the islands. And, by gosh, she was a fine-looking woman too if only she would stop keeping pigs and wearing yellow wellingstons.

It was midnight before she left, and the darkness was absolute.

'I'll be all right,' she told Hugh, 'I have my torch. You listen to your Mozart, if you wish to.' And in fact Hugh did this, till one in the morning. At that time he went outside. The sky was ablaze with stars, and he even saw some shooting stars, which astonished him. The music seemed strange in the house and he couldn't make out whether his mother was frowning more than usual or not.

*   *   *

Every evening after this she would visit him, and sometimes she would even come over in the morning. He found himself waiting expectantly for her, and if for some reason she didn't come he felt disappointed and empty. Now and again he would visit his mother's bedroom and stare down at the hairpins and meagre jewellery she had left behind her. Stella would hoover the house for him, clean the dishes, say to him,

'I'm not sure that you should keep that dresser. It looks to me as if it has woodworm. You should get rid of it.'

I can't believe it, thought Hugh. Here I am doing the Open University and also meeting this Englishwoman every day. It's all very odd.

He began to wear a tie, which he hadn't done before unless he was going out somewhere. Stella too began to dress in softer colours. Pinks and yellows were her best colours, blue didn't suit her.

She would tell him about her husband. 'He was a chemist, as I told you. But he would have long periods of depression in which he became very cruel. He would hide my things around the house and pretend I had forgotten where they were. No wonder I nearly went mad.'

She smoked heavily; the tips of her fingers were stained with nicotine. She was a compulsive walker about the house. Now and again she would rearrange a picture.

'That is awful,' she would say, 'really awful. I don't know who painted it, but it's dreadful. I could bring you some pictures, not of course ones I painted myself.' But Hugh insisted on some of them as well. One day she put up new curtains for him which she had found lying in a chest. 'Your mother has a lot of things,' she said. 'But I don't think you changed the curtains since she died.'

She told him about art as well. Vermeer was her favourite painter. 'His pictures are full of love,' she said. 'Love and light.' He found that he was understanding art and music much better than he had done before, since they were in fact part of Stella's

134   life. His marks improved. He even earned a B. 'Why, that's splendid,' she said, 'splendid.'

It was as if he was Columbus discovering a new world.

Alastair wasn't speaking to him at all, though now and again he would see him staring across from his garden, in the cold wind which had grown between them.

Alastair has nothing, he thought, and I have everything.

'You must, however,' said Stella, 'not neglect your own culture. After all, think of that lovely psalm-singing. I have heard it and it's truly beautiful. Eerie and beautiful. Like the sound of the sea.'

And he began to teach her Gaelic in return for her teaching him about music and art.

She was as apt a pupil as he was himself. One day she made oatcakes for him and he said they were very good, which they were, though he told her that not many people in the island ate oatcakes now. She even made a lovely dumpling.

'This is my mother's ring,' he told her one day.

'It's beautiful,' she said.

'You keep it,' he said. The ring had been removed from his mother's finger before she had been put in the coffin. He didn't know why he had agreed when the undertaker had suggested it, but he had.

'You keep it,' she said. And she kissed him.

It was then that he realised that he would ask her to marry him. Life was very full and precious. There was Stella and there was Hume and Vermeer and Charlotte Brontë. Images swam about the village from other countries, marvellously unique and costly and beautiful.

Stella's footsteps could be heard on the flagstones before she came to the door. Their heads were bent over books; she was learning while he played Gaelic music to her; she played Bach and Liszt. The house was a hive of industry, much more so than in his mother's day. He would find her shawl slung carelessly over

a chair and touch it gently. Death is very far away, he thought, 135
death is distant. Why should I think of it, though many others
on the island do. Also it turned out that she had a lovely voice
and could sing Gaelic songs with feeling.

Alastair continued with his poem about the Open University.
He added new verses. The third verse was as follows:

O gach feasgar agus madainn
bha mo liadh ag éisdeachd
ri ceòl anabarrach á Sasunn.
abair thusa céilidh.
An àite Gàidhlig anns an fhasan
bha Eadailtich ag éigheachd
am measg na soithichean 's na praisean
coltach ri na béisdean.

Every evening and morning
my good fellow was listening
to strange music from England.
What a ceilidh that was.
Instead of Gaelic in the fashion
Italians were shrieking
among the dishes and the pots
just like the beasts themselves.

His dislike of Hugh was now settled, for not only did he have
the Open University but he also had a handsome woman who
did not spend so much time with her pigs as she had done.
Everyone commented on her sudden radiance, on her dress
sense: of course she made most of her own clothes. Stella had
emerged like a strange flower from the common earth of the
village. Alastair seethed and seethed. Why, she would even smile
at him and speak in Gaelic. How cunning Hugh was! Of course
his father had been like that before him. He had clearly worked
all this out with long-term intelligence. He must have seen in

136   Stella what no one else had seen. Of course his father had had the first car in the village. Now he was proud as a peacock and doing well with his Open University too.

Stella insisted that Hugh go to the ceilidh in the village hall. Hugh didn't want to go, for he sensed that there would be something about himself on the programme. Furthermore, he didn't see many of the villagers now; they had become very distant. It was a tradition too in the village that any new event was celebrated, usually in a comic song. And certainly the Open University was an unusual and significant event.

Hugh listened to the songs and then saw Alastair stand up. Without looking in his direction Alastair began to recite his poem, which had become enormously long. The audience rocked with laughter. Hugh too smiled, determined not to appear ungracious or bad-tempered. Certainly there were hits against himself in the poem, the rhymes were better than ever, sharpened by Alastair's venom. Stella asked him what the poem was about and he told her. She too smiled and laughed at the parts which she understood. Alastair did not look at them at all. He was proud and confident. This was one of the best things he had done. There was prolonged and delighted applause when he had finished. Hugh made a point of congratulating him at the interval when everyone was eating cakes and drinking tea.

'That was a good poem,' he said, 'but you should have showed it to me first. There were one or two things I would have changed.'

'What?' said Alastair, taken by surprise.

'Just one or two,' said Hugh. 'You'll have to come to the house and I'll discuss them with you. This is Stella, by the way.' Stella shook hands with him gravely. 'I liked what I understood,' she said. Others came round and began to talk to them, as if now that the poem was over normal relations could be resumed. It was as if a balance which had been disturbed was now restored. And this was even more the case when Stella sang a Gaelic song which was received perhaps with greater acclamation than it deserved.

After a while Hugh saw Stella and Alastair deep in conversation. He was saying to her, 'Your pronunciation was not right in places. I'll have to explain to you.'

When the ceilidh was over, Stella and Hugh went out into the night engraved with stars. Around them was music and also the skies of Constable and Van Gogh. What a vast world this was.

'I think we should get married soon,' said Hugh.

'Of course,' said Stella.

They walked on in silence in a village that had become huge.

'I think that Alastair will visit us,' said Hugh shortly. 'He will make fun of your Gaelic.'

'That's all right,' she said.

'And we'll have to put away our pictures of the Virgin Mary. He thinks I'm a Catholic.'

'Poor Alastair,' she said. Poor Alastair, indeed, thought Hugh.

Maybe, he thought, I am cleverer than I thought I was. Maybe I did work out in advance everything that has happened without realising it. He looked up at the intricate forest of stars. Never had they seemed so bright, so challenging, so interesting.

ROCKAWAY AND THE DRAW

By A. L. Kennedy

She was thinking, only thinking. Because it felt good.

You can make someone deaf with a pencil. Just put it in their ear and shove.

Suzanne was feeling good and thinking and looking off and into the dark of a doorway, not particularly attempting to see anything, only looking off and entertaining thoughts.

Bang, bang, you're deaf. But why would anyone let you? And why would you want?

Ben progressed beneath the kitchen lintel and broke her line of sight. Ben was not the kind of man to walk. Ben simply and inexorably progressed within a familiar, steady range of speeds. She was used to thinking of his body bearing patiently down across the environment like tarmac, or a desert railway line. Ben would correct that to blacktop and railroad track, but she was used to thinking in English, because that meant she could remember who she was. Ben, of course, was Ben and in any language he would be broad and smooth as a gunsight, tempered and accurate. Whenever he came to a standstill anyone could be sure it was only because Ben had reached the most suitable point for the optimum comfort of Ben.

As he passed her, he patted her shoulder softly and unleashed a smile she still found unnerving. Some Americans simply had too many teeth, or too good, or too big – they were too obviously a later and better version of what the human being could be. They seemed almost dangerously well-prepared for feeding.

The human will and spirit are outstanding.

She watched as Ben snibbed a little door behind him and

left her alone with the passageway. Soon, she knew, Rochelle would come searching for her and make her enjoy herself again. Or maybe Ben had been sent to fetch her. She didn't mind. For the moment, she could overhear the party and contemplate.

The human will and spirit are outstanding. There are few trials that humanity cannot, given time, surmount. I know of a girl whose leg was taken all away by an alligator and she never even dreamed of giving up – neither during the ferocity of the attack nor later in the amputated quiet. If I was threatened by a thug with a pencil – a torturer with a pencil – threatened with being deaf so suddenly and simply – I would give up. With the alligator, too. With most things.

From behind the little door came the sound of flushing, a minor disturbance, the bubbling grind of a cistern, a pause. Ben unsnibbed and loomed forward, began approaching her with an odd intensity. When he paused and then gradually knelt beside her chair, she couldn't help but see his frown.

'Ben? Is something wrong?'

'Damn thing doesn't work right. Nothing I could do.'

'The damn thing . . .?'

'Doesn't work. It was there when I went in and it still hasn't gone. I don't know – nothing is any good any more. It's terrible. Are you coming back to the party, Rochelle thinks she's offended you, or you're sick, or something. It's her birthday and she's feeling isolated . . .' Ben softened his face into an expression so understanding that no one could mistake his attitude towards Rochelle for anything less than loving concern.

'Ben, it's not my fault she didn't invite any other women.'

'She doesn't like women. But she craves female company, it's a big problem for her. Please come back through.'

'I was coming anyway, I just needed some air and to think.'

'There you go with that thinking again.' His tone suggested he might be about to playfully ruffle her hair. He didn't. He didn't have to. She felt she'd been ruffled anyway.

'I'll follow you. But I need to . . . I've drunk too much

140 coffee.' Ben stood but failed to depart, doubtful. 'I'll be along. You go ahead.'

'Well, you remember it doesn't work. That thing had nothing to do with me.'

She smiled, not understanding, but smiling all the same in a poorly-nourished, poorly-hungry, European way.

And it was there; in Rochelle's bathroom, waiting; what Ben had found himself unable to remove and this was understandable, because it must have been more than equal to the average flush. Long, fat, solidly put together and the sweet colour of caramel, or milk chocolate or light brown shit, it swayed very slightly in the ceramic curve and shadow of the lavatory pan: a wonderfully monstrous light brown shit. But not Ben's. Not of his making. He'd been clear on that point.

As if in all these years, she'd never guessed why Ben went to the washroom, restroom, lavatory, toilet, WC. As if it had been a big mystery to her and always should stay that way. When Ben said he was 'going to freshen up' that was absolutely and only what he meant. He was going away for a while to become fresher; more soap- and cologne-scented; more agreeable to be with, although anyone would tell you that he was consistently agreeable in any case.

Ben had no bodily functions. He progressed and he loomed and he was perfectly attentive to all his acquaintances' mental states, and he was a good listener, one of the best, but he wasn't a bodily functions kind of man. Unless you counted screwing, although he actually had a way of doing that which made it seem no more than sporting, healthy and cathartic. You could guarantee catharsis with Ben. He found out *everything* you liked and told you *everything* he liked and then practised until both the sets of *everything* were as perfect as they could be. He constructed love faultlessly, as if it had never been a bodily function.

For the hell of it, she turned round after flushing and took a peek. All clear.

Back in the living room, the guests had arranged themselves much as she'd thought they would do. They were all around

Ben. He wasn't holding forth in any way but all the same, Ben was the heart of the room's attention. At the moment he was listening to Carter and Daniel and they were talking to him in the manner of charmed snakes, or medicated patients, or applicants for extremely substantial loans. Rochelle and Peter, Herman, Max, all chatted to each other convincingly enough, but if Ben had any need of their presence, even a tiny change of tone, or a modest call of beckoning laughter, would mean they delivered themselves to him completely. It would happen as predictably as nightfall. Ben was a draw.

Rochelle swirled her scotch up dangerously close to the rim of its glass and glanced at the door. She performed an exquisite double-take. 'Suzanne, are you okay? Ben said you were fine. But you're not tired are you? Are we being dull?'

With a pencil. Deaf.

'No, I'm fine. I was just getting some air. Things were peculiar at work today.'

'Well that's fine, then. Come sit with me.' Rochelle patted the space beside her on the bright, woven rug and Suzanne squatted obediently into position. Remembering how Rochelle liked to avoid any actual use of her furniture, Suzanne had dressed herself with an eye to reclining on floors. She had chosen a loose silk Indian-style trouser suit. Indian from India, not Native American. Had Suzanne dressed in the manner of a Native American, Rochelle would have offered her blankets and beads. That would have been her best appropriate gesture. As a British Citizen in the costume of a former British colony, Suzanne knew she still presented a tricky choice between a welcoming martini and a Wampum trade. Every time Rochelle observed her, they both heard the inexpensive tinkle of coloured glass.

'You sure you're okay? You look a little pale, dear.'

Rochelle, like many other people, treated Suzanne as if regular contact with Ben must render her somehow frail or sickly. Occasionally Suzanne would even catch herself pausing before a flight of stairs or stumbling through a sentence as if she really were an ambulant invalid.

'You don't have a drink, sweetheart.'

'That's all right. I'm not thirsty. Not right now.'

'Whatever you want . . .'

Rochelle turned back to Peter with a smile that meant their conversation could recommence. Abandoned to herself, Suzanne did not smile but examined the geometry of the carpet with some contentment while Rochelle settled in to ignoring her thoroughly. Rochelle ignored with flair; she did it with an élan and conviviality many people failed to exhibit in full-blown intercourse.

If you chose something stronger than a pencil, like a pilot pen, a powerful blow could force it clear into the brain causing cataclysmic damage, if not death.

Over by the draped baby grand, Ben was tilting his head to the left which meant he was trying his hardest to hear, getting a better angle on the sound, or the sense. Ben's surprisingly dark blue eyes were cold and open and hungry as an infant's while Daniel laced and relaced his fingers helplessly under one knee, his mouth letting out thin sentences with which his face patently disagreed. Carter seemed bewildered, but Ben was being generously intent. He listened the way a Russian icon listens; absolutely.

Under the piano in a nerveless sprawl was Rochelle's cat. Everybody knew about that cat. Something like a Siamese, it was expensive and took off for months at a time, leaving Rochelle distraught or sedated, depending on which of her doctors had gained her confidence. The cat had been christened Shelley, but people called it Prozac.

When Prozac was home it might sulk in the kitchen, or make an additional scratch of shadow in the margin of rooms. On some days it would circulate, screaming, at head height like a death-wall cyclist – nothing to keep it up and moving but the physics of speed and hate, or it might only bide its time, the ghost blue of its eyes willing an approach. Prozac drew blood. Prozac had put two people in A&E, one of them requiring facial sutures. If Prozac had been a dog, it would have been shot years ago.

Naturally Ben's favourite cat in the world was Prozac. He never would understand why nobody – even Rochelle – could like it.

'Here you go, Shelley, here you go.' Almost the first thing Ben did, 'That's a good cat, that's the best cat I know.' Standing in the hallway, not even stooping forward the way that anyone usually might to call an animal, Ben would murmur and smile and watch for Prozac, 'That's it. You're doing great. You're doing just fine,' until the little creature, because Prozac was only a little, mushroom-coloured creature, would stutter forward, stiff-legged, head low, tail breaking from side to side in an effort to be away from the man with the voice that was wires pulling over its skin. 'Good to have you back, Shel.' Ben waited until Prozac froze at his feet and then scooped her up like a scalp.

Suzanne would look at Ben's hands closing massively around the cat's particular arrangements of pelt and bone. Ben would close his eyes for a moment, perhaps concentrating, and Prozac's astonished body would suddenly fall into itself. Muscles lolled, its head dropped back to Ben's arm and a low purring began. Suzanne hated the purr. It made her nauseous. It made her think she had never seen every thought and independent intention so thoroughly drawn from a living thing. The effect could last for days.

So Prozac, anaesthetised and under the piano, would be perfectly safe to approach this evening, although Suzanne was careful not to go near it herself – she didn't like to take unfair advantage. She also remembered that in Prozac's gaze she could often see something not unlike despair.

'What are you talking about?'

Growling softly back home inside Ben's indecently spacious car, she discovered she had spoken out on behalf of the cat.

'I thought you might want to leave it alone.'

'Shelley? I hardly go near her. Are you jealous of a *cat*?'

Suzanne could almost see that last word, bouncing out in the darkness beyond the dashboard display. Its single syllable

144 had a greenish shine about it – the colour of gently teasing incredulity.

'I'm not jealous. I just don't think it likes to be held.'

'Oh, Suzanne, she comes to me. I call her over, she comes, I pick her up, she purrs. She wouldn't do that if she didn't like it. Come on now, lighten up.'

'I don't think it can help itself.'

'Yeah, look, I'm sorry you don't like Rochelle, but she does like you. We don't have to visit so often. And it does mean that she buys from me – a tiny picture, a talking-point lamp, something she'll enjoy, even if she thinks she doesn't care. Rochelle hasn't the faintest idea of what she likes unless *someone* helps her. All she thinks she's looking for is another way to spend her money.'

No one but Ben could make selling pointless objects to the impractically wealthy sound so much like a vocation to one of the lesser-known caring professions.

'I have some Lakota grave goods, they're very hard to get and I know that she'll love and enjoy them if I say she will. She needs that kind of help.'

'Maybe she should just invest in better plumbing.'

'Huh?'

He really did say 'Huh?' like a person in a strip cartoon. That one tiny noise could make him seem like her very own illustration.

Interpersonal relationships of long-standing and good growth have often been based on foundations that any impartial observer would find wholly inadequate.

'Suzanne?'

'I was thinking out loud. God, I'm tired. Are you tired?'

'Tired? Ten minutes, we'll be home. I don't want to hurry – the cold's making things a little greasy. I'm sort of tired. But not *so* tired. Are you *so* tired?'

There was a kind of orange shine, all along those last two sentences. Ben set his hand briefly on her thigh, ran his middle finger from somewhere slightly above her knee to somewhere slightly below where it wanted to be. One of Suzanne's more rhythmical body parts – the one whose peculiarities and demands Ben had made his particular study – gave a beat or so and then subsided. Ben was rapidly ceasing to be any kind of artwork. He felt nothing but three-dimensional. His hand withdrew to make the gear change he needed for a turn.

In perhaps half an hour's time, he would lick her wrists and suck at her earlobes and then quite systematically take her apart, shake out the beat he wanted and then bolt her back into sleep. While he performed their mutually agreeable overhaul, she would find herself holding him and being once again surprised that she could be so intensely loving with a man who was so little more than mechanical. Then one of his technical spot checks would find her arching and stretching herself against his strangely unattractive body with the ache he'd so neatly installed for her howling between her throat and that perfectly snug and moist little space he'd made for himself inside her.

At other times and in another country, that space had been her cunt. Ben called it his beaver. She supposed beaver was a nicer word than cunt. Ben's beaver. She didn't mind it being a beaver, she only found it odd that it wasn't hers. Ben's own genitals were quite attractive, but nothing on which she would wish to stake a claim.

In the thick, heavy unconsciousness that unfailingly followed Ben, Suzanne would dream. Arid, hollow-skied dramas would cyclone and suck around her, almost as if the impossible and usually tasteless bodily fluid she had learned to drink from Ben could guarantee both sleep and hallucination.

The Young Man arrives at the Rockaway Gas Station empty – without money, without belongings, without any visible assets beyond his smile. He has a wonderful smile that could persuade anyone of anything, but he only uses it to show he is contented. He is easily contented.

The Old Man takes the Young Man in. Although it is not in his nature to be sympathetic and this is made utterly clear from the outset, the Old Man takes the Young Man in.

146 *Perhaps the Old Man is lonely, perhaps he is affected by the Young Man's smile. Perhaps there is a sexual something here, bending in the mindless air that glistens out above the baking sands and bringing a faint but unmistakably mineral flavour to the mouth.*

For whatever reasons, the Young Man is able to move in and make himself a snug little space. He clears out the storeroom so he has somewhere to sleep and wipes off years of thirsty dust from the sad collection of sepia goods the Old Man has gathered to sell all available drivers who might ever happen to stop. Very few drivers are available or stop. Beyond the gas station there is nothing but panting death, air looping back on itself to hide from the heat, and the faintest suggestion of steel guitars. Nobody knows that inside the grey-boned gas station which looks to have been all over with and closed for decades there are twelve pairs of rubber overshoes – sizes assorted – brass bottle openers in the shape of naked women; baseball caps that commemorate the Mount Saint Helens volcano blast; jars of brown-coloured, home-made sauce suitable for shellfish; genuine pearl buttons; a matchbox full of human hair; knives made out of ground-down saw blades; two-pound boxes of lump sugar; a manual on wartime anti-gas protection: two hundred bright yellow pencils with eraser tips.

Suzanne noticed wakefully that the gas station partly offered the contents of her grandmother's kitchen drawers. Her grandmother had married in wartime, married a man who had no chance of living for more than a few weeks beyond their vows. Like thousands of others, she had flung herself on the mercy of the future and found it to be momentarily distracted. Grandmother's first and never-mentioned husband had lingered for a while in a hospital near Stratford-upon-Avon. He had been sad to discover the bomb blast had left him deafened and blind, unable to move. He had died calmly.

People do not die calmly because no one around them has time to be an adequate audience. People are simply courageous and courage is often refreshingly untheatrical.

Ben woke Suzanne and then woke his beaver at around nine a.m. She struggled slightly against his chest, still dreaming of horse skulls and dust.

'Ben?'

'Who else. Good morning. How are you?'

'Oh. Groggy I think. My God, we've slept in. Why didn't you wake me?'

'I just did. You've forgotten, haven't you?'

'Forgotten?'

'Today we're taking time out. Nothing to do but schmooz before I have to go away. It's the healthy thing to do. Now you rest for as long as you want to and then I'll fix you something good. It's been snowing since dawn. A lot. Picked the best day to stay at home.'

'How long will you be gone for?'

'Oh, two days – three at the most. Don't worry.'

Suzanne didn't worry, she waited until the bedroom door swung to and then slipped up from under the covers and walked to the window. Down in the street, everyone knew exactly what to do. Pedestrians slithered perfectly against soft sugar snow, leaping and tiptoeing the banks and reservoirs of icewatered slush at every kerb. Mr Beck from the fruit shop had bounced out a kind of mowing machine to chew up the hard packed surface in front of his store. His son was shovelling fragments neatly away. Seasonal changes were barely tolerated here, they didn't stand a chance. The subway gratings had already thawed themselves back to normality and monstrous pillars of steam were completely obscuring the roadworks at the far end of the block. The sky was set for a freeze, the palest, most merciless blue, but the city was still shifting, simmering under its surface, riding up on an invincible, buzzing heat.

In a desert place called Rockaway, the Young Man is trapped by the heat. It is plain that he can never leave the Old Man and the gas station unless something terrible happens first. He is given free food and lodging in return for his work, but there is hardly any work to do. His wages are subsequently very small. As each night swoops in below zero and shatters rocks, the Young Man owes the Old Man more money.

The Old Man doesn't seem to be so old now, not really old at all. Since the Young Man started waiting for him to die, the Old Man

148   *has coughed less and begun to shave regularly with a steady hand. The*
      Young Man has stopped smiling.

Had it been anything like a hot day, Suzanne would have
had to go walking with Ben and maybe sat in the park. Far
enough into the park and the ceaseless passing of traffic could
be mistaken for something like a tidal swell, or the wind in
a great many trees. Suzanne could sit on a bank or a bench
and convincingly picture the Thousand Islands and the Finger
Lakes where she and Ben had gone once when they were freshly
married and he did not yet know quite completely how to please
her. They had sneaked away to practise each other in a place
where they could concentrate.

And certainly they could concentrate out of doors, but they
couldn't be alone. If they both paused for too long with the
warm weight of Ben's arm laid out across her shoulders, or
tucked in at the small of her back, or in any other posture
they might attempt, then it would happen – the draw. As if
Ben had thrown out food, or called, or scattered pheromonal
substances by the handful, bird upon bird would come drooping
down. Every time she went out with Ben into anywhere like
the country, the same happy, Hitchcock rush would start. With
animals, too: everything wanted to be near him.

It was embarrassing. People would stop and look and then
they, of course, were also pulled on in. Ben would· squint at
the sun and scratch modestly through the hair just above his
ears while the grass quietly peppered with docile bodies. Dogs
would tug at their leashes, or trot freely forward until their heads
dropped and they lay down over their folded paws, oblivious of
any other calls on their attention.

Pigeons came the closest – like doves to Saint Francis, she
supposed. They were almost frightening. Completely silent
handfuls of breathing feathers, they watched Suzanne with
their golden-ringed, blood-coloured eyes as if she was the one
point in their world that was out of place.

Things like that wouldn't happen in Rockaway. No birds.

So she loved when it was cold and inhospitable outside their apartment. Today there could be no question of their stepping out and upsetting the balance of nature again.

A person, traumatically deafened, loses vital clues to his or her surroundings. The patterns and rhythms of reality subside. Moving into one room from another may be almost unbearable, walking out of the house, an impossibility.

'Let's take a walk.'

Ben frowned at her elbows where they leaned on the kitchen table. Suzanne made sure she kept them exactly as they were, even though her position was not entirely comfortable and seemed, in fact, to put an odd kind of pressure on her lower back. She knew that Ben's mother had kept both his elbows strictly under decades of savage control. Ben's elbows had never leaned, or even loitered. Even now, he could react quite oddly to certain expressions of physical ease.

'Suzanne? I said, let's take a walk. We can go to Reuben's, you like Reuben's.'

Every single thing she liked; he remembered them all. Yes to fellatio – if you don't shove; no to rye bread – however you hide it. Yes to cotton and 'Disaster Chronicles' and latkes. No to Gingridge, no to ragtime, no to lox. No to ever changing your mind.

'Reuben's. I don't know. They give you so much there, I hate to waste all that food.'

'Everyone gives you that much. We all eat over here, remember?'

'Yeah.'

'Come on. We can get dressed up warm and hold hands in our mittens, it'll be great. We did it last February, right? I didn't even think we'd have snow. Not this year. I'll go look for my boots.'

Ben preceded her down the front steps and onto the street. Up above, their apartment windows were a blank dark, as if there were no glass there and no successfully co-ordinated furnishings behind, as if where they lived had become an interval between floors.

150   The streets were trudging and stumbling with figures very much like Ben. Men and women wore ear bands and woollen hats, insulated parkas and rubber hoof shoes, as if this was their perfectly natural winter coat. They were nothing but sturdy and courageous. Although Suzanne was kitted out in much the same way, the hallway mirror had already proved she looked more than averagely out of place. She did not seem sturdy, only clumsily fat. Her hat reduced her face to imbecility while she wore it and when she took it off, she knew, it left her with an elasticated forehead scar one might very easily associate with recent and major cranial surgery. She didn't want to be outside like this.

'Come on now, better keep moving. Minus thirteen. You're not in motion, it'll bite. We've got time to make a loop – explore some.'

'You can't make loops here, you can only make rectangles.'

'Yeah. You're right. But you know what I mean.'

She didn't want to walk with him, but she did, all across Midtown and down into Murray Hill. The ice wind scalded her ears and made every colour ache and soar under the empty, frozen light. Suzanne sweated and slithered, oddly cosy between intersecting walls, the safe and solid slabs of Hudson River Gothic or blinding glass. Ben right-angled their route according to the well-patterned hopes of buildings that a New World, a world without conscience, loved to produce. An odourless death by refrigeration was snapping in wait for the unsightly, but there was nothing unsightly to be seen. All was suddenly, numbingly clean.

'Like to check out your favourite terminal?'

She would have liked to. Attentive Ben, considerate Ben, omniscient Ben, was right; Grand Central Terminal was somewhere she truly and unreservedly loved. She had never changed her mind about it, or grown tired of its peculiar, marbled intimacy. Despite its utter lack of visible trains, Suzanne had been nowhere quite so much to do with transportation. She could not walk into the concourse, look up at the clock, without feeling something pump underfoot. The whole place was a licking and breathing and hauling Westward compulsion. The indicator board alone could make her long for covered wagons, for a licence to drive recreationally, for anyway to be away and never mind if it ended in tears, if it always had ended in tears.

Among its many clacking revolutions, the indicator sometimes showed a train was due to leave for the best-sounding place in America, for Far Rockaway. It wasn't Far; only beyond the airport, out at the ocean's side, but she'd never been there. The idea of it was too lovely to risk visiting.

'Want to step inside? Out of the cold?' Ben began to steer her down Vanderbilt without waiting for a reply.

Pioneering and migrant hardships – forces which nourish a need for self-defence – have shaped the American character in both lovely and ugly ways. I am an immigrant. My hardships are negligible, but I may still learn to develop an interest in certain forms of personal protection.

'I'm not really all that cold yet, Ben. We can walk some more.'

'You don't want to go in? We're right there? It would be no problem. Are you feeling okay?'

'I'm feeling great. They've cleared the streets so well, we could get down to the Village and back.'

'Streets.' Ben squeezed her hand as if a wife who spoke a mildly different language was exactly the quality artefact he had been longing to acquire. But as they passed the Terminal building without a pause, he didn't speak.

'Ben?'

'Yes? We can turn back if you'd like. You want anything? Anything I can do?'

'Well, maybe if you let go my hand. There isn't really a path here for two of us side by side. Could you go ahead?'

Quick on the draw. In the context of pencils rather than pistols, this could still be a considerable threat.

'Yes, I could go ahead. Are your legs tired? You want to

152   stop? We could go back and get a coffee and fat-free cranberry muffins. You like them.'

'No. That's fine.'

Ben slid very slightly as he repositioned himself on the ice. He caught at her arm.

'Careful, Ben.'

'I'm fine, I'm fine. You do still want to go to Reuben's? Suzanne?'

'Oh, I don't know. I hadn't decided. I'm enjoying the walking so much.'

Attack need not always be attack, it can be pre-emptive defence. This is an American lesson and quite easy to learn.

'Ben, I was wondering—'

'What?'

'Have you ever been in a desert? Somewhere with sand and lonely highways and motels here and there, maybe gas stations.'

'Gas stations?' He was finding it hard to turn back and speak to her without losing his balance. Plumes of breath and heat moved around his head.

'Mm hm.'

'No, I'm a city boy. I was out in Akron once, that's about as far West as I've gone. One of the old tyre rubber families was clearing a house. For sure, there's nothing there, but it isn't a desert. Why? Would you like to see a desert? Vacation out there?'

Vacation in Rockaway. Alone. Come back with a pencil. Bang. Bang.

'No. No thank you. I didn't mean anything personally. I was only thinking.'

'You think more than anyone I know.' He tried a smile.

'I really can't help it. That's how I am.'

A VOYAGE

By Edwin Morgan

THE SPERM

In the beginning the sense of being was dim.
I do remember the first body, the man's,
Where I was herded haplessly with so many others
Through gloomy twists and ducts, till suddenly
I felt my own movement – like being born, that was—
As unseen vessels poured their milky fluid
Over us, and we swam for dear life—
Yes it was life, must have been – down
At first, then up that unforgettable tunnel
So narrow we were panting against one another,
Pushed onward, truly propelled, as long pulsations,
Shuddering contractions and expansions – what power!—
Shook the tunnel wall and drove us jostling
Into what I thought would be upper air.
How wrong I was! The explosion was volcanic,
The release, the scattering, the four, five waves
Were like the climax of some giant act
We were and were not part of. It had put us
In another place, another body, another tunnel
Enormous after the one we left, alien,
Acid, terrifying, formidable, wonderful!
What a sight we were! Imagine first
A revolution in some city square,
A million people gathered swarming, gesturing,
And then imagine four hundred such cities,

154 Drag them together like images on a screen
And watch the seething, struggling mass. Can you?
Can you count four hundred million souls? 'Souls'
May be pushing it, but you know what I mean—
The word slipped out, I'll let it stand. Well then,
We were there, in the woman, *in vivo*, in her caves
And galleries and underground streams, an army
Of explorers, aspirers, tunnellers, Galahads,
The living, the sick, the dying, and the dead.
You maybe think one sperm is like another,
But oh, not so, I can tell you. Acrobats,
Loonies, power rangers, Columbuses, moribunds—
I saw them all. In that first scatter-shot
They spread in such a monstrous tangled blash
Some never could swim free. I watched a trio
Twined together, sinking. There was a tailless one
Feebly shaking its head. One swam backwards.
Some wriggled or darted aimlessly. One broke in two.
Pieces and runts were scavenged by prowling cells.
Tidal waves swept millions out of sight,
Down, down and out, I've no idea where!
So life is tough, I thought, but on we go.

I swam strongly, up into the tunnel,
Learning that movement, quite as much as force,
Was what mattered. The head, like a snake's wedge,
Must weave from side to side, the tail must thrash
With rhythm, the whole body must trace
The five points of a star. As I looked around
Through the thinning millions, I was well out
In the vanguard, and cut quite a dash
(If you will forgive me) with my tail's
Obedient and flexible fibres, the fructifying bands
Of power-pack energy at my midriff, and oh
The treasure of the three-and-twenty threads
That throb, none broken, all perfect, in my head,

My hungry prow high-pointed towards the Other,
Which I shall find. Am I too confident?
I do not think so, though I know my rivals
Whom I see coming and going, never far
From the front, recognizable – did you know that?—
Some male, as I am, some female, I can tell them.
There's one I call Michelangelo, a bruiser
And no mistake, thickset, dour, powerful,
Swims in quick bursts, shaking head like a dog,
And dogged he is, I must watch him well.
His opposite is elegant to the last degree,
Thin, sleek, cutting ravishing curves
With her tail like a hair from the bath: I call her
Nefertiti, and she almost smiles.
Then there's Bonnie Prince Charlie, flighty
And slight, yet with an unmistakable flair
As he flirts his short tail like a kilt and steers
An unsteady but undaunted upward course.
My favourite, though, is one who might win home
Against the odds: she's hard as nails, she swims
Angular, awkward-seeming but not really so,
Her fibres and articulations shine
As she shoulders (you would *think* she had shoulders)
The seminal webs apart; I fear and like her,
She's my Sigourney Weaver. When I say 'like',
What do I mean? Could two sperms fall in love?
I am given to speculate, but there's no *time*.

I'm off. Cells are flying, waters weltering,
Strong contractions in the tunnel wall
Draw me along till I'm more boat than swimmer.
But that's too good to last. A sticky curtain
Guards the narrower paths and conduits ahead,
The caves and shafts and desperate isthmuses
We have to squeeze through, shedding companions
By the hundred thousand at each station.

156 Well, that gloopy mucous mass is push
And push and push again, with a special thrash
Of the tail and a mighty thrust and we are through.
I am through, that's the point! It is my story.
Poor Charlie slipped, what frantic pirouettes,
But then he lost all sense of orienteering,
Diminished, vanished down the lurid adits.
Onward the rest, potholers at the vestibule
Of caverns maybe measureless to man
But not to us! Into the penetralia!

THE EGG

Waiting, waiting, silent and still,
What I must fulfil, I will.
I rolled, I lolled, I oscillated
Along paths anciently created.
I'd love to say that I 'broke free'
From the sac that constricted me,
But no, I was expelled from it,
And though I knew I had the wit
To say 'I am', I only moved
When fleshy fingers had approved
Of me and pulled me in, and tunnels
Drummed me wetly forward, funnels
With bristles tickled me like a trout,
Dandled me about and about,
Fondled me into this resting-place
Where I can rock, and dream, and face
The butting heads and lashing tails.
What does nothing, yet prevails?
That's me, that's my magnetic power.
But times there are, in darker hour,
The prison of my sphere assails me,

And something like a teardrop veils me.
Oh to be truly free! but I
Must wait like an unsleeping eye.

THE SPERM

The caves are full of – what are they full of? – us,
Sliding waters, pulsing walls, wandering cells
But not the right one yet. How strange to think
This mechanism, this place with all its splendours
Interlocking, planned, crafted, long perfected,
Should be a cradle of adventitiousness
At our level, a rough chaos of sloughed
Cellular stuff and smurf, earthquakes of posture,
Din of irregular waters, fragments of things
You could not give a name to, an environment
That would faze all but the most intrepid:
Keep Piranesi, wipe the Taj Mahal!
The smaller you are, the more you see of its workings.
Not that I see myself as small at all.
I deduce it from the majesty of the voyage.
Well, it prepares us for the world outside!
Contingency keeps order on its toes.
I love it. I'm not complaining. My strokes
Are strong, in rivers murky or clear, I jostle
The debris as it judders past, I gauge
The turns and angles like a skater.
                                    Nefertiti
Is weakening, in her exhaustion her slow tail
Wags like a run-down clock, she's falling back
In a fading flaunt of beauty, a last tilt
Of that chiselled head. She's only one of many.
Where are the millions? Tight junctions loom
For a struggling hundred or two, a caravan
Of battered, flagging desperadoes kept going
By tinglings, breathings, scents and apprehensions

– Impossible, but there it is – of goals,
Ends, embraces, giving and taking of treasures—
They feel it, I feel it – let us press forward,
Brothers, sisters—

THE EGG

Not a wish, not a notion.
There really is a dim commotion
Quite near the cave. Is my waiting over?
Where is my sailor, where is my rover?
Nothing is easy: worst and best
Are still to come. Can you invest
My fort? You want drawbridge, doors,
You must try elsewhere. No floors,
Roofs, bells, stairs? What will you do?
I am not here to frighten you.
Well yes I am! but that's the way
To pull the hero into play.
Very slowly I am revolved,
As if my host had now resolved
To show me to the Argonauts
Alive, complete, and theirs. My thoughts
Are on another life to come,
Grown like a bramble, not a plum.
The walls tremble. Wash through then,
Nature, joy of gods and men!

THE SPERM

This is the chamber.
Something must happen. I was weary, but not now.
How many are left, a dozen? Cavernous is the word,
With many things dark, or stirring, half shining,
Shapes even here, though it is far more tranquil

Than the first tunnel, that seem made to disconcert.
What are those cells, lookalike bodyguards
For the one cell we want? And sperms like ghosts
From some earlier encounter, what are they doing
Still knocking at the door? Why don't they die?
And all those stains and trails, milky graffiti,
MENE MENE TEKEL UPHARSIN of the underworld,
Are they a warning, a welcome, a nothing?
                                           I swim
With broad strokes, further in, wondering.
Suddenly it is there, it, slowly turning,
The thing, the egg. My god but it is big,
More massive than I had ever imagined.
We circle it warily, as if it might bite.
But it is closed, baffling, aloof, impregnable—
At that joke I snapped out of it, looked hard
Across its surface, watched my companions,
Began to manoeuvre. I am not the first.
Michelangelo has breenged forward like a bull—
Finesse is not his forte – stubbed his blunt head
On the unyielding egg, broken his neck.
His body pieces twist down out of sight.
After so many adventures, it is grim
To see the death of the strong. Strength will not do,
I thought, or will not do enough. Surely
Sigourney would know, she would not fail.
Ah, but a fold in the cave wall released
A vicious alien, a sperm not one of ours,
Stringy with jealousy and disappointment,
Who fastens on to her and twines about her,
Dragging her struggles off into the dark.
Sigourney, Sigourney! I would have cried out,
But she is gone. Apart from a few stragglers
I am alone. What am I here for then?
Our host, this monstrous hustling watery dynamo,
Has purposes beyond our knowledge, not

160   Beyond our wonder, which is an early kind
Of love. Who would not tremble as that egg
Trembles? She guards it, yet she wants it entered.
I have to re-enact the very deed
That gave me life, I have to penetrate
The very flesh that drew me in before.
I swim up close, my head buzzes, ferments—

THE EGG

Now I feel a clear vibration,
And I tremble with elation.
What use is solitariness,
Mother only of distress?
I slid and surfed into this place,
Washing my daunting carapace
With waters that protect and feed
And keep alive the primal need.
Whoever knocks at my doorless shell,
Be bold, be hard, be sweet, be fell!
Nothing less mixed will force me to
Open my brooding heart to you.

THE SPERM

Close up, it's almost too big to be seen.
You have to fight your way through a waving wood
Of filaments, a crown of thorns, a cumulation
Of cellular fuzz and fuss, a *noli-me-tangere*
If ever there was one, but so what?
It whispers as you wade in. You don't believe
A word of it, and push. At last you see
The surface, the zone, shining, tough, pellucid.
You gather your energy, your head throbs,
And head body and tail flail in a frenzy

As you attack the sphere. God, I am there,
I am fixed, I am sprawled, I am crucified
Like a living fossil: can't stay like this!
How to get in? I never felt my jaws
– Jaws? why not? – so powerful, they eat,
They cut, they gnaw, they dissolve – revolve—
It's like a drill of enzymes – what an idea—
But it's oblique, more like a camel-bite—
A lively, deadly slit – you can almost hear
The zone sighing as you wriggle through—
Sinking into the universe of the egg.
I knew there would be change, but not this change.
My tail has lost its force, oh, all its service;
It snaps, it is gone, somewhere into the smush.
My body is crumbling, going, it is broken
As I am broken in this grainy blinding egg-white.
Its power-pack seems to have migrated
To my head, my beautiful jewelled snake's-head
Which grows and grows until it almost bursts
But doesn't yet, everything is fine, we lose
To gain. How do I know? I am slowly drifting
Towards the goal, the throbbing tingling packet
Of secrets, the egg within the egg, the twin
I have at last myself become an egg for,
To meet with till the two are one again.

THE EGG

Now you have no escape from me,
But I have ways to set you free.
Your three-and-twenty treasures lie
Swimming in a last joy with my
Three-and-twenty treasures, and
This is how we grow a hand,
Get a foot to walk the sand.
It is a grace to understand.

162 THE SPERM

My three-and-twenty treasures I freely give you.

THE EGG

Our six-and-forty treasures will outlive you.

SPERM AND EGG IN UNISON

May nothing ever, then or now, misgive you.

BURNING ELVIS

By John Burnside

I don't know why I choose to remember one thing, rather than another. Maybe whatever it was that happened turned out to be the myth I needed – the myth, or the necessary lie, which comes to the same thing: it's a Tuesday afternoon, early in the summer; it's already too hot and I've come indoors, into the shade. Idly, I switch on the television and start watching a documentary, something about America in the early sixties: JFK, the space program, the sad innocence of consumerism. It doesn't capture my attention, it's just background for a while – I even go out to the kitchen halfway through and pour myself a long, cold drink. I fill the glass with ice and mint leaves and carry it back, almost unbearably aware of myself as an isolated body in a closed space – and that's when I see her: a young girl in a light-brown uniform, with a scarlet cap, in a sun-bleached garden somewhere in Texas or Arkansas: a dark-haired girl with a bob, dancing, or playing hopscotch, half-aware of the camera. She's smiling – to herself, mostly – and she seems happy. It's not that she looks so much like Lindy; or if she does, the resemblance is superficial. It's just that smile, that sense of herself as a complicated game, and maybe it's the faded sunlight, the suggestion of a life beyond the film, a long childhood of beaches and Christmas trees that never really happened. When the programme ends, I stand looking out at the empty street: the suburb on a weekday afternoon, clipped lawns and pools of shadow, an astonishing stillness, that moment's sense of being alone, of turning around and finding the whole thing – the whole world – is a calculated illusion.

★

164 It was spring when the Andersons moved in next door. I first saw Lindy one afternoon, out beyond the fence, where the houses back on to the old nurseries. I used to go wandering out there to escape Mother's neatly manicured garden. You could still see the odd clump of irises, the rows of shrubs laced with bindweed, but mostly it was derelict and overgrown, with wide milky puddles in winter, and lush docks and nightshades in the summertime. I liked it there, I liked the way it had been reclaimed by wildness: the sheds collapsing slowly under the weeds and the rain; the tarmac cracking, shot with mayweed, the hedges blurring, everything running to seed. I didn't notice Lindy to begin with, but I knew someone was there. It was only when I climbed the bank and looked down that I saw her, sitting amongst the hogweed and nettles, smoking a cigarette. She looked up into the sunlight: a thin, lithe girl with short black hair, who seemed, in that first moment, almost unbelievably beautiful. She looked at me curiously, as if I was some strange animal she had met out there amongst the bushes and briars. There was a brightness in her eyes, a look of expectation that made me expect something too, but she didn't speak, she didn't even acknowledge my presence, she just took a long drag on her cigarette and looked away.

'I suppose you're the kid from next door,' she said at last.

I laughed. It was funny, her calling me a kid, when I was older.

'Do you go to Saint Mary's?' she asked and, though I didn't know her, I could tell she was being somebody else, a character in a film she'd seen, cool and distant, one of the untouchables. I nodded.

'I'm in the fifth year,' I said, pointedly.

She smiled.

'So what's it like?'

I shrugged.

'It's all right.'

She stood up and smoothed her dress.

'Well, I don't suppose it matters. One school's much like

another.' She looked me up and down, as if she was trying to memorise my appearance, then she smiled sweetly, and climbed to the top of the bank.

'You didn't see the cigarette,' she said; then she gave me an odd wave, and walked back towards the houses.

★

She must have started school the next morning. I didn't see her for a couple of days, then I met her on the street, walking home, and we started to talk. I still remember everything she said that first day, and on the days that followed. I remember everything she did, every move she made, the clothes she wore, the way she kept flicking her hair out of her eyes. After that, I started to hang around outside school, so I could casually walk her home, and we fell into a game, where she didn't notice that I had waited, and I pretended I'd met her by accident, outside the gates, or fifty yards along the road. Sometimes we'd stand outside her house and talk for hours. I used to wonder what her parents thought, but I needn't have worried: Lindy got to do pretty much what she wanted. Once, when it began to rain, she called out to me, as I walked away, that I should come inside next time. I remember clearly, even now, the absurd happiness I felt.

Lindy was thirteen. She was two years behind me at school, but she seemed older. She liked old Hollywood films, especially horror movies. She knew who directed what, and when; she knew the names and biographies of the actors. Her particular favourite was Gloria Holden, in the 1936 film, *Dracula's Daughter*. She'd talk about that picture for hours: the mysterious woman's desperate longing to be released from her dark nature, the way she would tilt her head to listen through the soundtrack for something she alone could hear, and that moment when she surrendered – the self-mocking smile, the fuzz of blood on her teeth, the slow glide to meet her next victim. Once I got to know her a little, it didn't surprise me that she liked that stuff. She liked to make a mystery of things. I sometimes had the impression she'd been thinking for years about questions nobody else even considered, and she'd moved away, into a parallel life, with its own incontrovertible logic. Half the time, I didn't understand a word she was saying. She pretended to know about science: she'd talk about microfossils, cosmic dust, theories of evolution. Sometimes I guessed she was making it up as she went along, but I'd be impressed anyway. Everything she said lodged in my mind, as if it were indisputable fact. Even now, things surface from time to time, and I realise it's all there, mingled with the memorised hymns, with Boyle's Law and the basics of topology, part of the seamless fabric of my schooldays, gathered up and put away, like one of those huge, crazy-quilts my mother used to make from scraps of left-over material.

We would meet at weekends, in the nursery grounds, out by the old potting sheds. It was damp out there, in the shade; you could smell peat and mildew, and something else beyond the currant bushes and the viburnums, a dark, fenny smell, touched with spawn and duckweed – something ancient, almost primeval, lurking in the remnants of orange boxes and peat bags beyond the rotting doors. We'd sit there on Saturday afternoons, suspended in time, separated from the rest of the world by a fine membrane of must and warmth. Mostly, she would talk and I would listen. Sometimes we argued about films or music. She'd tell me I was a snob, because I didn't like Hollywood: she said art films were good, but that wasn't why I liked them – she said I liked them because they were art films. She used to annoy me some of the time, to be honest. But most of the time, she would talk about things that bothered her, like who killed Kennedy, or what really happened to Marilyn Monroe. One day she started talking about Elvis, about how every fault was magnified in him because, for a short time, he had been perfect. It might not have mattered, if nobody had witnessed this perfection, but they had, and it had become a historical fact. She said the story of Elvis's life was like any other myth where the hero comes into being. Perfection can happen, but it can't last, because people don't want it to last.

They want a crucifixion; they want the phoenix. They want the idea but they don't want the person. If Elvis had died before he went into films, they would have loved him forever and unconditionally. But he didn't die. He lived and his perfection was corrupted. Whatever he did that wasn't perfect was seized upon with relish and disbelief by people who had never loved him anyway. She said fans didn't love their heroes, they just consumed them. She said anyone who had really loved Elvis would have helped him, by making him see that he was the phoenix, and he had to be burned. People think the phoenix story is about how everything that dies is reborn from its own ashes, but Lindy thought the real meaning was in the flames, not the ashes, not the rebirth, but the necessary burning.

I listened, but I didn't really understand what she meant. Elvis barely existed for me: I remembered seeing his films at matinees, when I was a kid; I had a vague recollection of contained grace, and a kind of beauty that seemed remote and aimless, like the beauty of the tigers at the zoo. I knew he'd died a couple of years before, but I couldn't remember when.

'There are people who think he's still alive,' she said.

'That always happens,' I told her. 'They said the same thing about James Dean.'

She gave me a disdainful look and shook her head.

'Elvis is different,' she said.

I didn't see how, but I didn't want to argue. When it came to stuff like that, Lindy knew what she knew; she had her own system of beliefs and theories that were too beautiful to doubt.

'He should never have gone into films,' she continued. 'John Lennon said Elvis died when he went into the army, but I don't think that's true. It was the films.'

She lit a cigarette and stared off into space. I already knew that look: the rapt gaze of someone who lived entirely in her own world, utterly self-contained, and quite unattainable, and I believe, even then, that I had a sense of what was going to happen. Maybe this is hindsight, but I don't think so. It

168   was subtle, and I couldn't have pointed to any one thing, but something about her made me suspect a complicity with what happened later. It was the way she smoked, the way she talked, the way she was never still, never at rest.

'What we have to do,' she said after a while, 'is redeem Elvis.'

I laughed.

'And how are you going to do that?' I asked.

'By fire, of course.' She turned to me and smiled. 'Do you have a camera?'

'Yes.'

'Come round to my house next Saturday. Bring the camera. I'll tell you about it then.'

'Tell me now.'

She stubbed out her half-smoked cigarette and shook her head.

'Wait,' she said.

*

The following Saturday I went over to her house at ten o'clock in the morning. It was a changeable day, but the light was good. I'd bought a new film, and cleaned the camera. It was an expensive 35 mm SLR that Dad had given me the previous Christmas.

Mrs Anderson opened the door.

'Lindy's expecting you,' she said. 'Go on up. It's the first on the left.'

Her room was a mess. The floor was littered with sequins and beads, battered toys, pieces of clockwork, dolls' heads, old apothecary's bottles marked *Poison* or *Acid*. There was a pinboard above the bed, covered with photographs and stills of old-time Hollywood actresses: Hedy Lamarr, Joan Fontaine, Louise Brooks, Gloria Holden. The only picture that wasn't a still from a film was the famous Vietnam shot, the one Eddie Adams took of a South Vietnamese general shooting a prisoner in the head. It was a page she'd torn from a magazine: the prisoner, a thin man in a check shirt, has his hands tied behind his back, and his face is twisted with fear; though he isn't looking directly at the gun, he knows how close it is. I heard later that the picture was taken at the moment the weapon was fired, at the very moment the bullet entered his head.

The other wall was covered with drawings that she'd tacked up casually with a strip of sellotape; some were rough sketches, others were finely detailed, but they were all beautifully executed. They were also bizarre. A few showed scenes from old horror movies, but most were drawings of Elvis. The one I remember best showed him in his prime, in a black leather jacket, a sneer on his lips, his hair unruly. The face was beautiful, alive, arrogant – but under the jacket there was no body, only a set of ribs and a spine, and a white pelvis fading away into nothingness at the edge of the page. It's hard to describe – it sounds like the morbid imaginings of a teenage girl but for me there was more, a surprising poignancy, a glimpse of vacuum. Lindy told me she'd made that drawing on the night Elvis died.

The effigy was sitting in an old leather armchair, next to her desk, dressed in a cream-coloured jacket and black jeans. I didn't know then who it was, of course: the head was a blank – no face, no hair, just an old sack crammed with straw. Except for the clothes, the figure she'd made looked more like a guy for Bonfire Night than anything else.

'What's this?' I asked.

Lindy smiled mysteriously and went to the bedside table. She took something out of a drawer and walked over to the dummy, keeping her back to me, so I couldn't see what she was doing.

'Finished,' she said.

The dummy had become Elvis. It was wearing one of those masks you could buy from joke shops, the kind that covered your whole head, and just had pinholes for the mouth and eyes. It looked quite realistic, I suppose, for a piece of moulded rubber.

'It's not that great,' Lindy said. 'But it doesn't matter. By the time we're taking the pictures, it'll look like real.'

I nodded, but I wasn't convinced. As far as I could see, it was as good a likeness as it was going to get.

★

Lindy's mother went shopping around eleven. We waited till she had gone, then we hauled the effigy through the house and out the back door. Or rather, I did. Lindy carried the camera. On the way, she ducked into the shed at the end of her garden, and emerged carrying a large red petrol can.

'We'll need this,' she said.

As we walked, she explained the plan. We would take Elvis over to the potting sheds, where no one would see. Lindy had found a stake out there, which we would use to support the effigy while it burned. When it caught fire, I had to start taking pictures, and I couldn't stop till she told me. I was pretty nervous. If somebody came, it would be difficult to explain what we were doing. They might think we were starting a real fire. Needless to say, I did all the carrying. Lindy walked on, a few paces ahead, talking non-stop, to keep me distracted, so I wouldn't chicken out.

'Did you know Elvis had a twin brother?'

I didn't answer. I was holding the effigy round the waist, so the mask was a few inches from my face; every time I took a step, the legs banged against my knees and I had to keep stopping to get a better grip.

'It's true. His name was Jesse Garon. He was stillborn, I think. Or maybe he died soon after he was born. Elvis's father put him in a shoebox and buried him in an unmarked grave, somewhere in the woods in Tennessee.'

She kept talking till we reached the potting sheds, then she found the stake and pushed it into the ground. She pulled some twine out of her jacket pocket and I helped her tie the effigy to the stake, so it was almost upright. The top half of the body slumped to one side, and she fussed with it for a while, till she got it straight. It didn't look much like Elvis to me; it didn't look like a person at all. Lindy had tucked the top of the mask into the collar of the jacket, but there was still a brown patch where the sacking showed through, and there was something less than life-size about the figure, a slackness that reminded me again of the guy at a bonfire. Still, Lindy seemed happy enough.

'Is the camera ready?' she asked.

I wound on the film and offered it to her, but she shook her head.

'It's your camera,' she said. 'You do it.'

She took a good look round and, when she was certain nobody had seen us, she splashed the effigy with petrol. For a moment it shivered, as if it was about to fall, then it burst into flames as Lindy tossed a match and leapt out of the way.

'Go,' she shouted.

I started taking the pictures. Seen through the lens, the burning figure looked more real, more like a person. Amidst the smoke and flames, the mask became a face, and I moved in closer, as the body twisted and crumpled, trying to catch the image of burning flesh that was almost visible for a moment, before the material blistered and fizzled away. It was incredible. It couldn't have lasted more than a minute or two, but I really believed I had caught a glimpse of the real Elvis, the Hillbilly Cat, the Elvis Lindy wanted me to see.

'All right,' she said, as the body fell and started to burn out. 'We've got enough pictures.'

I turned and looked at her. My face was hot and flushed from the heat of the fire, and I felt exhilarated. All of a sudden, I understood what we were doing. I understood everything. I looked up: small white clouds were drifting across the sky, but right above my head there was a gap, a patch of deep, mineral blue, like the colour of lapis lazuli when it is moistened and warmed by the breath. I felt dizzy. At that moment, there was no way of distinguishing between

172   me and Lindy and this patch of sky. Everything was seamless.
       I looked at her.
           'This is amazing,' I said.
           She shook her head and smiled sadly.
           'Let's have a cigarette,' she said.

                                    ★

Memory is something mineral, a deposit that builds up over
years. It has nothing to do with the past; it's entirely a matter
of what is wanted in the present. Yet I'd like to believe, in
some objective way, that that was the happiest summer of
my life. Burning Elvis had created a complicity between us;
I felt we had shared something, that we were similar, bound
by a common spirit. I started smoking, to keep her company.
We would meet by the sheds: Lindy would bring a packet of
Sovereigns, and we would lie on our backs, staring up at the
sky, smoking and talking. I suppose I'd begun to think of her
as my girlfriend, though neither of us had ever said or done
anything to justify the assumption. I wanted to touch her; I
wanted to kiss her face; I wanted to unbutton her blouse and
stroke my finger lightly along the ridge of her collar bone. She
would wear a short blue skirt with white polka dots. Her legs
were golden; her thighs and arms were covered with a soft
silvery-blonde down that I ached to touch. But I never did.
Maybe I knew she would refuse me: the only way I could
keep alive my fantasy that we were virtual lovers was to stay
behind an invisible line that she had somehow drawn between
us, without a word or a gesture that I could recall.
    One afternoon, towards the end of the holidays, we were out
on the other side of the field, sitting in the lowest branches of a
spreading maple tree. There was a pause in the conversation and
I looked at her. It was the one time I came close to crossing the
line, and Lindy must have read my mind, because she slipped
to the ground suddenly, and looked up at me.
    'Do you know Kiwi Johnson?' she said.

'Who?'

'Kiwi,' she repeated. 'Kiwi Johnson.'

I nodded slowly. I remembered Kiwi Johnson all right: he'd been in the fifth year when I was in lower school, and I didn't like him. Nobody did. He was one of those boys you see in the corner of any playground, pretending he isn't there. I could tell, just by looking at him, that he thought he was different from the others. He wasn't excluded, he just didn't want to join in. In games lessons, when the captains were choosing teams, he was always one of the last to be picked, not because he wasn't any good, but because he resisted selection. Whenever a team captain looked in his direction, he would stare back coldly, as if he was daring the boy to choose him, and the captain would move on, taking Pig Lee, or Specky Aldrick, rather than face that malevolent gaze. It made people resent him. Usually, if a boy was picked towards the end, because he was fat or effeminate, or generally despised for no good reason, he would run into line quickly, grateful to be chosen at all. Those boys were always on the alert, ready to accept without protest their apportioned share of humiliation. They knew they were despised: they were always fussing, trying to appease everyone at once, making silent promises with their eyes, to try harder, to be what was wanted. Kiwi Johnson stood apart from all that. He made it clear that he didn't want to join in – if it hadn't been for the teacher, he wouldn't even have bothered. Yet when he was forced to take part, he played with a cold, deliberate brutality that surprised everyone. It was a kind of challenge. In one football game, Mr Williams made him play forward, instead of his usual position, at left back. About halfway through the period, someone accidentally passed him the ball directly in front of the net: he paused a moment, looked at the opposing goalkeeper, a small, wiry boy called Manny Doyle, then he punted the ball straight at his head. It was a cold, wet day. Our year was out on the other field, about a hundred yards away, but we all saw Manny go down. Later, he said it was mostly his fault – he'd seen the ball coming, he just hadn't ducked in time. Kiwi didn't say anything, he only glanced round at Mr Williams, as if to say, *now look what you've made me do*.

I used to wonder how he got the name Kiwi. It wasn't a nickname: there was no affection in it. There was no real venom either, but it was still an expression of dislike, like some of the names we gave to teachers, and nobody used it to his face. Once, Des Coffey followed him around the playground, taunting him, and they were obliged to fight. People who remember nothing else from school can still picture that December afternoon, the week before the holidays. In those days, we had rules; there was an underlying code that prevented anyone going too far, so the damage was always more imagined than real. But this was one of those occasions when the rules might not hold, and everybody was excited. Nobody had ever seen Kiwi in a fight before, but most of us thought Des would win. He was in Kiwi's year, but he was much bigger, and a famous dirty fighter.

The two boys met outside the gates and fought for fifteen minutes in a drift of falling snow. Usually, when a fight happened, there would be gangs of followers egging their boy on, urging him to acts of viciousness that were never serious possibilities – *smash his face, kick his teeth in* – that kind of thing. But this fight was conducted in total silence. We just stood there, awed, as we watched the first real battering we had ever witnessed. When it was over, Kiwi walked away with a handkerchief pressed to his mouth, but Des Coffey had been punched and kicked so systematically he was almost unrecognisable. Quite a few of the spectators were friends of his, but nobody lifted a finger to stop the punishment. That was another part of the code. Everybody knew it was stupid, but nobody questioned it. If you called somebody out for a fight, you accepted the consequences.

Now Kiwi would be nineteen, maybe twenty. He'd left school at the end the fifth year and as far as I knew he was working at Scandex, making gaskets. I'd seen him in town, on a motor bike: he wore a cutaway Levi jacket and had lurid tattoos on his hands. He'd been in trouble a couple of times, but I couldn't remember why. Now, I looked at Lindy in amazement.

'Kiwi Johnson?' I said, with obvious distaste.
She laughed.
'Have you seen his tattoos?'
I was annoyed now. I didn't know what bothered me most, that she would be interested in someone like Kiwi, or that she would tell *me* about it, as if I was some girl friend from school.
'I think he goes out with Cathy Gillespie,' I said.
'Well he used to,' Lindy said, looking pleased with herself.
I dropped out of the tree and stood facing her.
'And?'
She laughed again.
'And what?'
'Why are you so interested in Kiwi Johnson?' I said, realising I sounded like the jealous boyfriend I wasn't.
'Why shouldn't I be?' Lindy answered coolly. 'He's interesting.'
I felt sick. As far as I was concerned, Kiwi Johnson looked like one of the bad guys that Elvis was always beating up in his films. I started to walk away, thinking Lindy would call me back, and tell me it was all a joke – she didn't like Kiwi at all, she was just pulling my leg to see what I would do. But she didn't. I got as far as the bank before I stopped and looked round. Lindy was standing under the tree, lighting a cigarette. As far as I could tell, she had already forgotten I existed.

*

That was the end of an idyll. As I remember it now, I still saw Lindy every day, but she was remote from me, neutral, preoccupied with something. I had no doubt she was thinking about Kiwi; I didn't think she was going out with him. But towards the end of the holidays, I learned different. I'd met Lindy in town: as always, whenever I was with her, I was totally absorbed, the rest of the world might not have existed for all I cared, and I didn't know anybody was there until, with an odd,

176 almost imperceptible shift, I felt Lindy detach herself from me.
I turned and saw Kiwi and another bloke, a tall thin guy with
straggly henna-coloured hair; the two of them were listening
with mock-seriousness to whatever it was I had been saying.
A moment before, Lindy had been with me, now she was with
them, and there was a gap between us. I was the outsider, and
Kiwi knew it. He took Lindy's arm.

'We're going over to Dave's place,' he said. 'Do you want
to come?'

'Okay,' Lindy said. She didn't make any move to free herself,
to make him let go of her, and I realised it wasn't the first time
he had touched her. I was disgusted and fascinated. In all the time
I'd known Lindy, I'd never touched her, not even accidentally.
There was a kind of unwritten law about it, a zone around her
body that nobody was supposed to enter.

Kiwi glanced at me and Lindy turned guiltily. I knew she
would have left me there, if he hadn't intervened.

'How about you?' he asked.

'I don't know,' I answered. I didn't want to leave Lindy with
them, but I didn't want to go to Dave's place either.

'You ought to come, too,' Kiwi said. 'You should take a
look at Dave's pictures. Did you know Dave was a painter?'

I looked at Dave, helplessly. There was no way out, without
looking like an idiot, or a coward. Dave grinned, and we went
to his place.

★

I only remember the first part of that afternoon. Kiwi offered
to read Lindy's palm, while Dave took me into another room
to show me his pictures. As I remember them now, I have to
admit they were very good, in spite of the subject matter. Dave
showed me the book he'd used as a source for most of them –
some specialist text on crime-scene forensics, with full-colour
plates showing murder victims in a variety of poses: a woman
tied and gagged, with her throat cut open; a man with his face

shot away; what looked like a teenaged girl, with one leg cut off just below the knee, and both hands cleanly amputated, the look on her face a mask of unimaginable horror. The paintings were huge: the stylised figures they portrayed were obviously drawn from the photographs in the textbook, but they had been subtly altered. All the pain had been leached away and what remained was like the end of a game, or a ritual: the figures were not so much victims as icons.

I looked at Dave.

'Don't say anything,' he said. 'I don't want you to make any comment. All right?'

When we got back, Kiwi was studying Lindy's hands as if he really understood what he was doing. Of course, I knew it was a sham: he was aware of me all the time, he could see it annoyed me that he was touching her, that he could so easily form an intimacy with her from which I was excluded. Lindy was joining in; she seemed to take him seriously, attentive to everything he said, murmuring agreement from time to time, elucidating, confirming, asking questions. It offended me that she could believe the lines in her hand contained some arcane text that only he could read. It didn't matter that it was all an act, what mattered was the complicity between them, the way she allowed him to elicit memories and confessions with his carefully open-ended remarks: a history she hadn't thought to share with me, she offered casually to him, because he was special, he was the gifted one.

Dave made some coffee. When Kiwi had finished with Lindy's palm, he offered to read mine, knowing I wouldn't agree. I felt my refusal was taken as an evasion, as if I were afraid he would discover a secret I preferred to keep hidden, something I would be ashamed of in front of Lindy. I remember wanting to leave and not knowing how; then, before I really knew what was happening, Dave took something out of a box and started cutting it up with a razor. He kept looking at me and smiling, then he put something in his mouth, and handed each of us a tiny particle of what looked like dirt. I watched Kiwi take his

178   piece and put it on his tongue, then Lindy did the same. They were all looking at me, smiling, almost friendly, waiting to see what I would do. I put the grain of dirt in my mouth, and let it dissolve. Lindy smiled and kicked off her shoes.

I didn't feel any effects for about half an hour. Dave put on some music and started talking to me, but I wasn't really listening. I heard Kiwi say to Lindy that he liked the pictures: at first I didn't know what pictures he meant, but then they started talking about Elvis and I realised she'd given him the photographs I'd taken at the burning. I was angry. Dave was talking about the Nazis: he started showing me pictures of young women from some Hitler youth organisation: they were performing gymnastics or playing games with hula-hoops, all tall and slender and unimpeachably Aryan; Dave told me how he'd seen films of these women when he was a kid and he'd been obsessed with them ever since. I was trying to hear what the others were saying – they seemed to be arguing about Elvis's father, arguing and laughing, touching one another from time to time, exploring, entering and retreating, establishing something. On the other side of the room, they suddenly seemed far away; Dave kept talking, flicking through the book and confessing to me how these were the only women he liked, these blonde Hitler girls in their white shifts. I couldn't tell if he was being serious.

After a while, my body began to feel warm and a little tight, as if my skin had been stretched, like the surface a drum. I remember a moment's panic, the thought that something would snap, like a piece of catgut, then I let go and relaxed. Time had slipped. I was alone in the room now, but I could hear voices. They were close to my face, only inches away, whispering softly, almost unbearably kind, all the people in Dave's paintings, whispering through great pain, merging one into another, into a single, multi-threaded voice.

'*Come home now.*'
'*Listen.*'
'*You know where you are.*'
'*Come in. Come in.*'

'Listen.'

Then another voice came through the haze, much clearer, a voice I recognised but couldn't put a name to.

'I'm waiting for you,' it said. 'I won't let you fall.' Then I saw Dave, sitting on the edge of the bed.

'Are you okay?' he asked.

I nodded.

He reached out to stroke my face, and I drew back in alarm.

'Where's Lindy?' I almost shouted. It didn't sound like my voice, it sounded like one of those others, one of those people in the paintings.

Dave bent down and kissed me on the forehead. I stiffened and lay still, with my arms at my side.

'Don't worry, baby,' he said. 'Take it easy.'

He laughed softly.

'There will always be a father.'

*

I caught a trace of the smell as soon as I opened the door. It was stronger in the hall than it was in the porch: a smell of damp clothes, an old coat, or a jacket, saturated with dirt and rain. I thought someone had broken in, and I hesitated – what if he was still there, in the dining room, or somewhere upstairs, startled by the sound of my key in the door, standing still, holding his breath, waiting to hear what I'd do next. I listened. It was a long time before I dared to push open the dining room door and look inside: the smell was even stronger now, and I couldn't understand it – it was definitely the smell of stale, wet clothes, but how could the intruder be wet, when it wasn't raining outside, when it hadn't rained for days? I walked through to the kitchen. The back door was open and there, on the threshold, I saw a naked footprint, just one, dark and perfectly defined on the light cement. I froze. I knew who it was had been there. I don't know how, but I did, and I wasn't

180   afraid: I felt as if I'd just received a secret message, or a sign, and it had something to do with the drug Dave had given me. It was a riddle that I'd been set: now, all of a sudden I knew how to solve it. I slipped off my shoe and placed my foot over the print. It was a perfect fit, just as I'd expected. I smiled then, and shook my head. It didn't matter now that everything was out of focus. It didn't even matter about Kiwi. I was happy; I understood everything; it was my life that was happening, nobody else's. I walked across the garden and climbed the fence into the nursery grounds. I was certain he was out there, hidden amongst the shrubs, crouched in the long grass, waiting for me. It was hours before I gave up the search.

*

I didn't see Lindy till after term started. I felt bad: I couldn't remember where she'd gone that afternoon at Dave's flat. I couldn't even remember how I'd got home. That day had ripped a hole in my life, in everything I took for granted. I pretended to my parents that I had a summer cold and stayed in bed for a couple of days, to try and collect my thoughts. Then, even when I did see Lindy, I didn't know what to say to her. I had convinced myself that she was part of some plan to humiliate me. I thought she had worked the whole thing out with Kiwi and Dave: the drugs, the voices, even the phantom footprint. It was all her fault.

    For her part, she hardly seemed to notice me. She existed in her own space, and I began to understand that I'd never had anything more than a marginal place there. I used to imagine that knowledge was the beginning of change, but I suppose I've always known that there was too little between me and the rest of the world, that I'm all surface, all availability, and I haven't been able to change that. I'm still the same as I was that day, when Dave and Kiwi showed me how remote I was from the centre of Lindy's world. Looking back, I understand now how unaccountably gentle they were, how what I took for a cruel trick on Dave's part was really a bizarre form of courtesy. He wanted me to see that I was different in kind from people like Lindy and Kiwi, that they were fearless in a way I could never be. I was too attached to myself, I wanted to understand too much, to always know where I was. He was letting me know that it was all right, that there was nothing I could do about it, but at the time I only felt ashamed, as if I'd discovered a flaw in my soul, a weakness I would never overcome.

A couple of weeks later, we were playing *Judex* at the school film club. It was the first show of the new academic year and I was involved in organising the event. As a conciliatory gesture, I caught up with Lindy on the way home and asked her if she wanted to come, but she just looked mysterious and told me she had something else on.

'Really?' I said, trying to sound casual. 'Anything interesting?'

'I'm going out.'

'On your own?'

She paused, partly for effect, partly because she hadn't decided if she wanted to tell me.

'Well, not that it's any of your business,' she said. 'But I'm going out with Kiwi. On his bike.'

I'd suspected that, but I must have looked hurt nevertheless. Lindy shook her head.

'Don't be a drag,' she said. 'It's just a bike ride. Anyway, you don't know what he's like.'

'And you do I suppose?' I was more irritated than I had meant to sound.

'Yes.'

She stared at me with that sublime assurance of hers, and I knew it was too late to change her mind.

'I like him,' she said.

I didn't speak. By now I was wondering how far it had gone. I had a sickening flash of Kiwi's hands, with their blue and scarlet tattoos, poised at the hem of Lindy's dress. I even had an ugly, fleeting idea of them together, and Dave watching,

182   in that room of his, filled with pictures of the dead. I turned away, so I wouldn't have to look at her.

'God,' she said. 'You don't understand anything.'

I looked back at her. I wanted to sound neutral, with a hint of older and wiser, but it didn't come out that way. Even to myself, I sounded petty.

'I just don't trust Kiwi Johnson,' I said. 'And if you had any sense, you wouldn't either.'

She shook her head again. She seemed sad.

'I can look after myself,' she said quietly. 'Don't worry about me.'

'I won't,' I answered. I was ashamed of myself as soon as I said it, but it was too late by then. Lindy walked quickly to her door and let herself in without looking back, and I just stood there, watching her go, telling myself I didn't care anyway, sick to the stomach with jealousy and self-disgust.

*

I didn't go to the film club. It was a windy night, with occasional gusts of rain blowing through the cypress hedges and rustling against the windows like fine sand. Dad was away, and Mother was upstairs, locked in the secret room of a migraine. Whenever she got one of those attacks, she was distant and silent, as if she wanted to reduce her presence in the world to an absolute minimum.

I was restless. It sounds like the wisdom of hindsight, but I really did believe something bad would happen. I had a book open on the table, but I couldn't read. I kept glancing up at the circle of streetlight outside our gate and the darkness beyond, at the small white blur of the Andersons' porch lamp, and the privet hedges glistening under the fine rain. I didn't see anyone. Later I asked myself a hundred times where Cathy was all that time. She must have been waiting somewhere for Lindy to come home. She might have been standing outside our house for hours, hidden in the shadows, but in all that time, I didn't see her. Kiwi dropped Lindy at the end of the street, so her parents wouldn't know who she was with. It turned out later that they thought she was over at my house. She'd walked into the circle of lamplight outside our door, and Cathy had met her, silently, bringing the knife up out of the shadows. It must have happened while I turned a page or glanced at the clock – by the time I knew anything about it, it was over. It was a quarter past eleven. Somebody made a sound – not so much a scream as a half-finished cry – but I didn't recognise the voice as belonging to Lindy. I looked out of the window and I saw Cathy Gillespie under the streetlamp, just outside our gate. She was looking at something on the ground.

I ran out. Lindy was lying face down on the pavement. She was still moving – I think she was trying to get up – and she was making a low, gurgling sound in her throat, as if she was choking on something. Cathy had stabbed her in the neck: there was blood everywhere, on the hedges, on Cathy's clothes, all over the pavement. I couldn't move. Cathy was standing beside me, holding the knife, but I made no attempt to get it off her, or to help Lindy. I think I already understood it was too late.

The night was still warm, in spite of the rain. The privet was in flower and I caught the faint, vanilla taste of it through the smell of the blood. It bothers me now, that I can remember it all so clearly – to think that I was so aware of everything, yet still failed to act. I should have run back indoors and called for an ambulance. I should have tried to give her the kiss of life. I suppose I was in shock, but I still knew Lindy was dying. I remember thinking it: there was something about her body – she seemed smaller than before, less substantial, as if some essence had already begun to drain away.

I don't know how long it was before I heard the siren. That was the first time I became aware of the voices; someone had his hand on my shoulder and was telling me to go back inside. I turned and saw Mr Carpenter, from across the street. Someone else was holding Cathy by the arm: it was a man I didn't really know, who lived a few doors away. Cathy had dropped the

184   knife, or someone had knocked it out of her hand – it had a long, pointed blade, and a black handle. She had probably stolen it from her parents' kitchen. The man who was holding her was wearing a dressing gown and a pair of grey woollen slippers. In the light from the streetlamp, I could see that the slippers were splashed with Lindy's blood.

*

I saw Cathy in the Town Centre three weeks after she got home. It was about four in the afternoon: she was standing in the market square on her own, smoking a cigarette; she looked nervous and lonely, and I caught myself feeling sorry for her. She had the look of someone who's come back to a place and found it changed beyond recognition, inhabited by strangers who don't even speak her language or live their lives by the same landmarks that she once knew. She was looking at the people passing by: she paid special attention to the school kids gathering at the bus station – it was as if she had forgotten that seven years had passed, and all her old friends were grown up now, with kids of their own and jobs at Smiths or Scandex.

I stopped and watched her for a while. She didn't notice me – or if she did, I was as much a stranger to her as the other people in the square. Or not a stranger, so much as a phantom. It was some time before I realised she was waiting for someone, and I went on about my business. She must have been stood up, because she was still there, in the gathering twilight, when I came by later, with my bag of groceries and an armful of library books. I was pretty sure that, whoever she'd been waiting for, it was somebody who knew her from the old days. Nobody else knew who she was and I think that frightened her, as if the whole thing had been a dream, or the story of something that hadn't really happened. I wondered if she understood the futility of her actions. In all her life – in my life, too – it was the one defining event, the moment that stood out, and it could never be repeated. Now we were folding back into time: Lindy was dead, Kiwi had gone off somewhere, and she was standing there, smoking another cigarette, waiting for someone to turn up and make it all real. I suppose I could have performed that office; I could have walked over and spoken to her. Just to say her name would have been enough: she wouldn't have to recognise me. All she needed was for someone to remember – it would be like that moment when Dracula's daughter passes the empty mirror and the audience sees who she is. The worst thing about a secret is to be forced to keep it forever. People will kill for the sensation of being, just to see themselves in the story. Lindy used to say that everybody wants to be special; but Cathy wasn't special at all, she was nothing. Her fragment of history had passed and nobody knew or cared who she was. Life had moved on. It was a banal and surprisingly comforting thought, and all of a sudden it made me unaccountably glad, like the stillness of a city graveyard, or the first thick fall of snow, that obliterates and renews everything it touches.

SINGING MRS MURPHY

by Duncan McLean

Rug   I am not fucking your wife.

Shuv   Come on.

Rug   Fuck off.

Shuv   Just once, that'll do.

Rug   Get to fuck you radge, do you think I'm daft? Well you're fucking sick.

Shuv   Sick's got fuck all to do with it you stupid cunt. I mean I'm not asking you to fucking *enjoy* it – fuck all chance of that to be honest, that's half the fucking problem. I'm just saying we'll get her bevvied right, parafuckinglytic, you stick your cock up her and BINGO I jump out with the camera.

Rug   You're a fucking pervert, man.

Shuv   (*Laughs.*) Well I reckon you must be fucking bent, you cunt.

Rug   Fuck off.

Shuv   Here's a chance to get your hole, and you're turning it down! I'll tell you, I'll even buy the drink! A bottle of Buckie for her and a few cans for us – not too much, we want a fine big stiffie in the pictures.

Rug   You're fucking . . . out of the park, man.

Shuv   Am I fuck.

Rug   Aye, cause I told you: you don't have to go through this rigmafuckingrole these days. No one's fucking caring if you want divorced. You just get a lawyer on to it, blah blah blah, three weeks later there you go – mutual fucking consent.

Shuv Ah, but, who gets the kid?

Rug Eh?

Shuv This is it, you see. I'm not needing Kelly away with her – she's an old fucking alkie! What kind of mother's that for my daughter?

Rug What, and you're a better mother, are you?

Shuv Aye! So I've got to prove she's fucking unfit, right, bad morals and that. Step one: photos prove she's a slag, shags any cunt. Her defence: 'He led me on your honour, I was drunk.' We jump in: 'She's *aye* drunk, she's a fucking alkie, your honour!' Case closed!

Rug No way.

Shuv Come on.

Rug Nuh.

Shuv I'll pay you. A tenner. (**Rug** *looks away.*) Twenty!

Rug Forget it.

Shuv (*Pause.*) You are a poof.

Rug I'm not going to do it.

Shuv When was the last time you shagged somebody? A woman.

Rug Women are nothing but trouble, man. Give me a wank any day of the week.

Shuv Give yourself a wank you perverted bastard!

Rug Nah, but you ken what I mean.

Shuv (*Laughs.*) I ken.

Rug You ken?

Shuv Aye. Pure fucking hassle merchants. That's how I'm needing divorced, see?

Rug You should never've got hitched in the first place.

Shuv Aye well.

Rug Aye well?

Shuv I was young. My tadge was twitching. You ken what it's like at that age.

Rug What, you fucking past it now?

Shuv Ah . . . fuck. (*Shakes his head.*)

Rug 'Hold on to my zimmer while I get it in, hen.' Ha!

Shuv	(*Pause.*) Anyhow, what the fuck you talking about, man? It's you who's fucking past it or something.
Rug	Eh?
Shuv	You're the one that's not up to the business, by Christ! Too much tugging, man, that's it: you've rubbed and rubbed till you've rubbed it away. 'Ta-ra! The amazing disappearing cock!'
Rug	I'd give you a run for your money any day, you cunt.
Shuv	Why all the worry then? (**Rug** *shrugs.*) You're feart she compares us! (*Pause.*) You sad wee fuck.
Rug	It's not that.
Shuv	Either that or you are an arse bandit.
Rug	Not that.
Shuv	What then?
Rug	Nothing.
Shuv	Come on you bastard.
Rug	Well . . .
Shuv	Fucking *what*!
Rug	She's a dog.
Shuv	Eh?
Rug	Sonia, she's a fucking dog, she's bowfing. I wouldn't piss on her if she was on fire.
Shuv	(*Pause.*) What did you say?
Rug	You're well shot of her, I tell you man. All that yellow fat bulging through the fishnet tights . . .
Shuv	You! (*He jumps on* **Rug**, *wrestles him to the ground.*) That's my wife you're fucking talking about!
Rug	What are you fucking doing?
Shuv	(*Pinning him to the floor, knees on arms, leaning over his face.*) Don't you ever talk about my woman like that again.
Rug	All right, man, all right. Get off my fucking arms, will you.
Shuv	I fucking . . . married her, right . . . and no cunt's going to . . . call her names . . . when I'm fucking breathing.
Rug	All right, all right, I'm sorry. (*They relax slightly.*) She is fucking mauchit but.

188

(**Shuv** *hits him hard on the face.* **Rug** *is shocked for a second then starts to struggle. He wiggles his shoulders and bucks his hips trying to get* **Shuv** *off. Eventually he makes a big effort, and flings him clear.* **Shuv** *tries to make it look like he's got off of his own accord, and steps away calmly.* **Rug** *remains lying there.*)

Shuv   You're a stupid cunt. That's your problem, pal. Always has been. You have to ken when you're beaten, and you never do. And that's fatal, cause you're beaten most of the fucking time. (*Pause*) You have to be able to admit it: 'Right, that's me fucked.' And then you can make a fresh start. Pick yourself up, start from the bottom, climb: you can only go up. (*Looks down at* **Rug** *lying on the floor.*) But see your problem, man: you never admit you're fucked, you're always floundering about down in the shite and the pish and the puke, and you're grabbing folks' ankles, shouting, 'Nothing wrong with me pal, I'm doing fine,' and then you get another boot in the chugs and you're down in the dirt again. (**Rug** *grunts.*) Stop flailing about man, stop shouting out: then get back on your own fucking feet.

Rug   Cunt . . .

Shuv   What are you saying?

Rug   (*Struggling to sit up.*) Do you have to be so fucking rough all the time?

(**Rug** *crawls to the front, collapses, moaning. Shuv looks down at him, smiling, almost laughs.*)

Shuv   Come on, pull yourself together.

Rug   (*Rising up slightly, looking around.*) See's a drink then.

Shuv   Ah, you're a hardy bugger right enough. (**Rug** *collapses again.*)

(**Shuv** *starts looking around, picks up various cans and bottles, shakes them. He finds a few dregs, drinks them himself.*)

Shuv   Afraid you're out of luck, mate, nowt left.

Rug   Aw fuck.

Shuv   I could get you a glass of water.

Rug   (*Sitting up.*) I'm not feeling that bad.

190　　　(*Both laugh.* **Shuv** *takes out a comb and starts combing his hair.*)

Rug	What're you doing?
Shuv	Raking.
Rug	Oh. What for?
Shuv	See my skull? It's a fucking fanny magnet.
Rug	There's not much fucking fanny about here.
Shuv	There will be at the party though.
Rug	Is there a party?
Shuv	Too fucking right there is.
Rug	Whereabouts?
Shuv	I told you.
Rug	No you never.
Shuv	Aye I did. You've just forgot. (*Laughs.*) Jesus man, you're already a thick bastard, now don't go losing your memory as well.
Rug	Well remind me then.
Shuv	Oh, you coming are you?
Rug	What? If you're going of course I'm fucking coming, you cunt!
Shuv	You weren't invited.
Rug	(*Onto his feet.*) Since when has that fucking mattered?
Shuv	Ah well . . .
Rug	Come on you cunt! I'm dying of thirst here, bored out of my brain – it's Friday night!
Shuv	And you're young, free and single – or if not free, then pretty fucking cheap.
Rug	Too fucking right man – two cans of Hootch and I'm any cunt's!
Shuv	Right, smarten yourself up and we're off then.
Rug	Great. (*Puts on jacket, shrugs: he's ready.*) So where is this party?
Shuv	Pilrig Street.
Rug	(*Thinks: draws a blank.*) Who bides there?
Shuv	Fuck knows – I heard these two gadgies talking about it in the paki.

Rug   So nobody's actually asked you?

Shuv   Since when has that fucking mattered?

Rug   Suppose. (*He hacks, looks around, picks up a bottle and gobs into it, missing slightly.*) Still: it would be nice to be invited someplace. Sometime. Ken?

Shuv   We are invited! We invited ourfuckingselves!

Rug   Or how about us having a party? You and me. We could do it here: get some drink in, and eh, a load of drink . . .

Shuv   No way man. No fucking way.

Rug   How no? It could be good. A bottle of Buckie, a few cans . . .

Shuv   No fucking chance pal, and here's why: more than likely you'd get gatecrashers, mad cunts coming in and trashing the place.

Rug   Oh aye. Like us.

Shuv   And I just got it fixed how I like it. (**Rug** *looks around: the place is a fucking dump.*) Right, I'll have a slash and then we'll nash, okay? (*He leaves.*)

Rug   (*Shouting after* **Shuv**.) Here, we could get a stripogram. Aye! The party's in full swing, then this bird in a raincoat comes in, starts doing a fucking strip! Jesus aye . . . big tits . . . fucking ada! Right there by the bed. That close you could reach out and . . . anything, *anything*. (*He pictures it.*)

Shuv   (*Coming in, doing up his spaver.*) I had a stripogram back here once before.

Rug   Aye? When was that?

Shuv   Oh, six month ago.

Rug   I don't mind that, was it Hogmanay or something?

Shuv   Naw, just one Saturday there was fuck all on. I was fed up with the boozer and I hadn't got my hole for a while. So I phoned this agency, told them I had a stag night or something, ordered this fucking French maid. Anyway, a couple hours later there's a knock on the door. 'Where's the party then?' she goes. 'The party's about to begin, darling. Just me and you, ken what I mean?' And guess what?

Rug What?

Shuv She buggers off! Away down the stair without so much as a flash of her gash!

Rug Jesus Christ.

Shuv Fucking atrocious, eh?

Rug What . . . did you think she was going to strip off and let you poke her?

Shuv Aye! These fucking stripogirls, man – going round to somebody's house and doing the whole fucking raunchy routine – what do you think? They're not exactly fucking nuns, are they?

Rug (*Pause.*) You can get them dressed as nuns though, eh?

Shuv (*Pause.*) Aye. (*Both laugh. Then* **Shuv** *looks at* **Rug**, *and dives at him.*) Come on mother superior, show us your rosaries. (*They struggle.*)

Rug Get off me, you tit.

Shuv You love it.

Rug (*Pushing* **Shuv** *away.*) Come on, let's go.

(**Shuv** *grabs* **Rug's** *leg, cowps him with a thump, then stands over him, preventing him from getting up, as he speaks.*)

Shuv There's something we need to sort out first. What about dosh for the bevvy.

Rug What about it?

Shuv Well I've got fuck all . . .

Rug . . . for fuck's sake . . .

Shuv . . . what about you?

Rug Where do your fucking funds go, man?

Shuv Empty your fucking pockets!

Rug No way.

Shuv Right.

(*He dives, sticks his hand in* **Rug's** *trouser pocket.* **Rug** *fights to get it out. They struggle for a while.* **Rug** *appears to be winning, but then* **Shuv** *trips him up and leaps on top of him, pinning him down.*

They stare at each other for a few moments, getting their breath back,
then **Shuv** *speaks*.)

Shuv   Sing Mrs Murphy.

Rug   I won't. (**Shuv** *immediately slaps him*.)

Shuv   Sing Mrs Murphy!

Rug   (*He starts singing, unenthusiastically*.) Take it in the mouth
Mrs Murphy. (*Pause*.) It only weighs a quarter of a
pound. (*Pause*.) It's got hairs all round it like a turkey.
(*Pause*.) And it spits when you rub it up and down.

Shuv   (*Grabbing Rug's head, pulling it in towards his groin*.)
Again!

Rug   Take it in the mouth Mrs Murphy.

Shuv   Louder!

Rug   It only weighs a quarter of a pound.

Shuv   Fucking LOUDER!

Rug   It's got hairs all round it like a turkey.

Shuv   (*Slapping* **Rug**.) COME ON!

Rug   And it spits when you rub it up and down.

Shuv   Yeaaahhh! (*He leaps up, strides about, shouting*.) Fucking
Mrs Murphy, you cunt – what are you?

Rug   I don't ken.

Shuv   Fucked! (*Pause*.) You're fucked and you know it. (*Pause*.)
Good! Fucking brilliant, you cunt! Fucking well fucked.
But at least *you know it*: knowledge! (*He looks at Rug for*
a second, still lying there, then goes over and grabs him, hauls
him to his feet.) Come on, get up! Get up, verse two!

Rug   I don't ken it.

Shuv   (*Sings, shaking Rug by the lapels*.) I will ride you like
a badger.

Rug   I will ride you like a badger.

Shuv   Yes!

Rug   I will ride you like a stoat.

Shuv   COME ON!

Rug   If you suck upon my tadger.

Shuv   (*Shouting right in* **Rug's** *lug*.) I will cut your fucking
throat. (*He flings* **Rug** *to the floor again, then strides about*

for a while, exultant. Then he turns back to him.) Give us your dosh.

(*Beaten,* **Rug** *gropes in his trouser pocket. He pulls out a hanky, and a bunch of coins come out with it and scatter across the floor.*)

Shuv   Stay!

(**Shuv** *picks up the money, goes to a clear piece of floor away from* **Rug,** *starts to arrange the cash into piles. After a while, Rug props himself up on his elbows.*)

Rug   You're fucking out of the park.

Shuv   Holding out on me, you cunt, eh? Right, let's see . . .

Rug   (*Starting to get up.*) That's mine.

Shuv   You stay where you fucking are! Don't move a muscle or you're fucking dead! (*Stares him out.*) Now, four pounds . . . one fifty . . . four tens . . .

Rug   That's to last me . . .

Shuv   Shut it! One five . . . eight twos . . . and ten fucking one bastarding pences. A total of . . . five twenty one.

Rug   Aye, and that's to last me till Thursday.

Shuv   (*Jumping up.*) That'll get us a bottle of Prince Charlie's Barley Bree from the paki.

Rug   Can I get up now?

Shuv   Four ninety-nine a go. Pretty fucking good for this day and age. I mean there's not many places you get whisky under a fiver.

Rug   I'm getting up now, okay?

Shuv   Right enough, it's pure fucking battery acid, but still: does the job, eh? (*Walks to the door, giving* **Rug** *a shove as he passes.*) Did I tell you to get up, you cunt? (*Pause.*) Well, come on, get your fucking arse in gear, are you coming or no?

Rug   (*Pause.*) I'm not coming.

Shuv   (*Pause.*) Well you're not staying here. This is my place.

Rug   I'm not staying here.

Shuv   Well if you're not staying here, and you're not coming out, what the fuck are you doing? I mean where the fuck are you going?

Rug Nowhere.
Shuv Nah. That's where you are: nofuckingwhere. Here's where you're going: up my wife's cunt.
Rug (*Pause.*) Wherever. (*Getting to his feet.*)
Shuv Too fucking right. (*He heads for the door.*) Come on, cunt.
Rug (*Pause.*) Okay, prick.

KATHLEEN JAMIE

Pearl

  Perhaps I began
like a pearl, unwanted
dirt soothing itself
on the sofa, *swine*,
growing round, pale,
cushioned in upholstery
month by month, as in pregnancy,
then years. 'Her indoors',
I call myself. Empress of flesh,
in printed smocks, hearts
and flowers. A weekly
wheely-bin of shame, Pot-Noodles,
Wotsits, poverty stuff, till my walls
the labouring stairs, at least
would hug me.

And I filled rooms, as churches
are replete with God,
But God's nothing, a wraith.
I'm greater than that, cathedral
in skin, pillars of fat
beneath my breasts, heat
where my thighs chafe. I press
one heavy-lidded eye
to the curtain's chink,
this harled house, a goddess walled.

Some nights I lie, breathless,
imagine fossils, ammonites coiled:
my vitals, spine, heart
flattened in strata of fat
– and sweat, I could slice me
with a bread-knife, free
and cradle my struggling heart . . .

I was a lass
like any other: big boned,
same drunken rows. In gran's
sticky kitchen, she'd lick her thumbs
'ignore them, sweet-heart.' Butter
scones, she nourished me,
then died. The wonder is what they endure:
arteries, spleen
before, like a cartoon bedspring
burst . . . 'Tub o' lard
eh?' is what I gasped
to the fireman; ha ha, sick
fairy-story joke. A competence
of men swarming up my stairs, Welcome!
to the boudoir of the princess
beautiful, men
slickly removing windows, the rush of air—

I cried
when I saw the crane's clawed winch
framed in my window, waiting
to swing me wrapped
in a pink sling
like a stork brings a lovely
baby; but not this public
caesarean: I heard the gasp,

even the traffic hushed
for my moment's

198   apotheosis, terrible
      rooftops, a tugging wind.
      Gran! Please,
      Give 'em the V's, girl
      The world and his wife; ambulance, fire-engine.
      Let me die, now. A gang of neighbours clap

      hands to their mouths
      as to streets half forgotten
      I'm revealed: a gross vision
      of Our Lady: 30 stone.
      out of control, let herself go, poor cow, don't stare
      their thin peasant whispers
      rise to me like prayer.

The Garden of Adam and Dot

The garden blooms under the eye
of the terrible Dot;
she casts out all beasts,
especially cats, with a broom, saying *Ah'll choakit!*
and Adam snaps shut the wicket-gate
and his black briefcase,
awa tae the Masons
with just a daft pinny
to cover his shame.

The Flower-Sellers

In the gardens
of their mild southern crofts, their
end-of-the-line hillside vineyards,
where figs turn blue, and peppers dry
strung from the eaves,
old women move among flowers
staked in their yards; each

with a worn knife, a sliver
crooked in the first finger
of her right hand—
each, like her neighbours
draws the blade
on to the callus of her thumb,
so flowers, creamy dahlias,
fall into their arms; the stems'
spittle wiped on their pinafores.

Then, when they have enough
the old women
forgather at the station
to await the slow, busy little train
that will take them to the city,
where families drift between Mass
and lunch, and they hunker
at bus depots, terminii
scented with chrysanthemums,
to pull from plastic buckets
yellows, spicey russets,
the petally nub of each flower
tight as a bee;
and from their pockets, pink ribbon
strictly for the flowers.

We must buy some,
though they will soon wither,
from this thin-faced
widow in a head-scarf, this mother,
perhaps, of married daughters
down at the border—
or this old woman, sat
among pigeons and lottery kiosks
who reaches towards us to proffer
or grasp
the morning's fresh blooms;

200   or the woman there, who calls 'flowers!'
in several languages—
one for each invasion:

We must buy some,
because only when the flowers are dispersed
and carried upwards
to apartment blocks' third or fourth floor
will the old women feel ready
to make for home, beyond the suburbs;
each with her neighbours,
back where they came, with their
empty buckets and thick aprons
on a late-morning train.

Extract from
AN OUTLYING STATION

a work in progress

By Alan Warner

One night, Christmas, year of the big freeze, when Varie Bultitude was seventeen and wavering, stoned in white stilettos up the track that led to Broken Moan, she came upon her wheelchair-bound father's dead pale face below vertical moonlight, eyes and mouth wide open, false teeth missing, head thrown back defining his windpipe; his penis was in his lap, fascinatingly entombed in a small, spectral amber ice-block of his own urine; infinite frost crystals festering on his blackened cheeks lit by moonshine and blue stars, then, in a direct and graceful sweep, a lone satellite crossed the big sky above.

Old Bultitude's arms hung behind the muddied tyres, his torso was welded solid into the wheelchair that had become hopelessly jammed on the rough track, the right wheel wedged in a frozen mud rut, the left solidly sealed in an outrageously large, rock-hard cow turd.

Varie finally screamed and began up towards Broken Moan, stumbling, kicking aside one white stiletto and further round the curve another, then running on until, with a loud crack, her heel came down on her father's upper plate of dentures which shattered under the stocking sole then drove shards of plastic into the flesh of her soft left foot.

At dawn in the freezing fog that had lifted off the New Loch, Doctor Drumvargie came lurching up the track towards the big house in his Range Rover. He stopped behind the police Land

202 Rover which was parked, blocking the track, then, taking his bag with him, he continued on foot. Even the doctor stopped to goggle as the rigid, military-upright corpse of his patient, Andrew Bultitude, emerged from the fog, flanked by the dark uniforms of Sgt. MacPherson and a constable. When the ambulance headlights materialised down the track, the men prised the corpse forward and it broke free of the wheelchair. A square plate of frozen urine-ice stuck to the seat of the pants then fell to the track. Balancing carefully, the two ambulance men negotiated the corpse on a stretcher down the verge of the track.

After the ambulance had slowly reversed back towards the main road, the combined efforts of the doctor, the sergeant and the constable couldn't budge the wheelchair. The constable chipped away with an axe from the Land Rover and only managed to burst the tyre. Finally Sgt. MacPherson relented; kneeling reverently, he emptied the hot contents of his morning flask on to the big cow turd; a foul brandy-&-coffee-scented steam rose off it and soon the shit turned runny enough to tear the wheel free and pull the chair out. The doctor lifted up his bag and walked off into the fog towards Broken Moan, the big Bultitude residence.

In the large, dark kitchen a policewoman was sitting silently with the Bultitude girl who was slouched in an old armchair by the Aga. As soon as the doctor arrived, the policewoman nodded and stepped outside into the fog. Straight away the compromising and ugly exchange with Andrew Bultitude's daughter occurred but was soon followed by the disinterested reward of the perfect and brilliant whiteness from the plastic, top-front-left tooth the doctor eased with tweezers from deep within the lacerated heel of the Bultitude girl's soft teenage foot with its ankle chain and painted nails; the instant the tooth pulled free from a strand of viscous, dark blood, the doctor thought of the luminescence of toothpaste-froth spat on a black docken leaf under a moonlit sky when he had camped out with his own daughter the previous summer.

With a zing the doctor dropped the tooth into the enamel milk jug among the other bloodied shards he'd picked out. Strange: it was the top-front-left tooth that was knocked from the Bultitude girl in that horse fall, replaced by a single false tooth and pink roof-of-the-mouth plate, fitted by a fine Glasgow dental practice the doctor had himself recommended to her father. This single false tooth was the solitary blemish on the girl whose head lolled from side to side after the two injections. Doctor Drumvargie stood and wiped his hands. Varie's left stocking had been ripped up to the hem of her short skirt and a shred of the black nylon hung vertically down, almost touching the linoleum; the doctor's wide fingerprints of dried blood were up to just above the knee – but no further – where he had steadied the leg while working away at the foot.

The doctor crossed to the Aga, moved the big blackened old kettle from the hottest plate and used both hands to pour himself a mug of instant coffee, then he draped a tartan rug over Varie, sprawling in her dead father's favourite armchair. He heard the grush of the police Land Rover pulling up in a curve outside.

'That's where the bugger was headed,' Sgt. MacPherson nodded. He pointed downhill into the freezing fog, away from Broken Moan. The black track seemed to lift up to its own reflection in the steady vapours. Off to the right they couldn't see the edges of the New Loch, then the fog would cave in, showing smudges of young birches. The female constable nodded at MacPherson. From within the fog the other constable pushed a wheelbarrow requisitioned from the gardener's outhouse towards them; the barrow was loaded with bottle-shaped presents in the livid pinks and reds of wet Christmas wrapping that with the touch of a finger would smear aside to reveal the honey clarity of glass and cheap blended whisky.

'They were buried under the snow before the main road,' the young policeman called but just then the three turned to stare at a dark figure seemingly walking on the water over the New Loch's surface straight at them out of the fog banks, a stooped

204   man with the face of Christ, wearing a white shirt and a yellow kilt (surely a woman's skirt); two orange-coloured gardening gloves clutching a carrier bag to each thigh, he crunched over the broken puddles of the track then scowled with one dead-seeming eye at the strange sight: a policeman with a wheelbarrow of Christmas presents, the two white, mud-stained stilettos next to a lower set of dentures resting on the bonnet of the police Land Rover, the empty wheelchair. The man let out a knowing snap of a laugh then launched himself up the landward side of the banking beside the track, vanishing into the blades of reed grass clustered together in frozen clumps; then came the heavy squeak as he crossed the rusty fence marking the end of the Bultitudes' property and the start of open mountainside.

'Loch's frozen,' grunted the Sgt. He turned to the two young constables, neither were natives. 'Tell you. He's been using the same paths for years. He's like a train of ants. Before the glen was flooded by our man here' (he nodded to Andrew Bultitude's lower dentures on the bonnet), 'Man Who Walks always used to cross the Glen and the Bultitude Lands here. In '75 Man Who Walks comes down off the Ben side there and since he hasn't done this route for a month or so you can imagine his dismay when he finds a new loch in his way – where the hydro's flooded it yon water is only about ten foot deep but your boy must've been fair flabbergasted to come across it but Man Who Walks thinks nothing. He grabs up a dried-out giant hogweed stalk, clutches the biggest rock he can lift and just walks into the water, across the bed of the New Loch then out on the shore at this side – just the tip of the giant hogweed stalk sticking up, like yon things off submarines, that he was breathing through then away up the mountainsides.'

The Sgt. coughed, clapped his gloved hands together. 'Andrew Bultitude designed the dam up on the mountain, the turbines inside it, the dam at the end of the pass, and the flooding of this glen that meant the submersion of the village down there, the village that Bultitude and his family lived in. His old mother

owned all the land anyway so he made good business selling the
lands to himself.

'After the dam was completed at the far end of the pass, the
water level slowly rose over the fields and village. Everybody
had left – the council-house folk up to the new estate out at
Java And Jericho – but in the big Manse house on the hill,
Bultitude's old mother refused to leave – her best furniture
was man-handled up the wide staircase to the first floor then
eventually on up to the top floor away from the daily-rising
inundation. The old woman was using crazy Scorgie who's a
salvage diver out on the island now; he would swim down into
the kitchens to retrieve a beloved copper saucepan or whatever
and old Mrs Bultitude, sleeping on these rafts of forty-five gallon
drums that Scorgie had built, rafts which rose closer and closer to
the ceilings each day, Scorgie, who'd become her guardian, and
Mrs Bultitude, playing *Monopoly* and surviving on tinned soups
off a camping stove; in daylight hours, Scorgie rowing reporters
from newspaper and telly, rowing them from room to flooded
room in a bright orange dinghy for an audience with old Mrs
Bultitude, imperial as you like in her red velvet armchair on
a raft. Niall Duibh, the poet who lives out at Little Australia,
was a visitor, he wrote a poem about it describing *Conch shells;
water-reflections gesticulating on the crumbling ceilings*, then the day
when the Yank, Nam the Dam, who's got his own old chopper,
winched her off (they call him that because he served in Vietnam
then recovered in Amsterdam), aye, Nam the Dam winched the
old woman off the roof, up into the air she went from beside
the chimney, the rising waters on to the roof slates by now and
Mrs Bultitude's tiny, tiny feet marching in the air below Nam
the Dam's Westland whipping up the surface of the New Loch,
Scorgie swimming through the spray, off eastwards, downstream
with a new current, chasing the red velvet armchair (the rest of
Mrs Bultitude's floating furniture was by then pressed against the
ceilings of the topmost rooms in the Manse, below the surface of
the New Loch). Those were the days of The Floating Church
when the insane priest, McBain, protested against his submerged

206   steeple with its sickle-carrying, stooped weather vane on top: that was the final part of the village to sink below the surface, even after Mrs Bultitude's chimney pots, then in heatwave weather as the New Loch level fell, Death can be seen walking on the water's surface towards the west at dawn and McBain would row his church barge with its balsa-wood replica of the sunken steeple, preaching along the banks of the New Loch, dropping anchor just offshore of the farms and dwellings along the new shoreline, often all the water-facing windows shut to McBain's imploring voice over the dawn water as . . .'

The Sgt. walked into the kitchen. The doctor stood smiling, warming his arse on the Aga. The wealth was everywhere – in the casual untidiness, the piles of green wellies with dried mud on them by the door, the copper cooking pots hung along the mantle, the technical drawings of the hydro designs framed in wood on the walls, that indefinable smell of the kitchens of the rich that the Sgt. had recognised over the years; spices, dogs, curled lino and the big worn armchair that spoiled little bitch (though she stood as tall as the policeman already) was sprawled in with her bandaged foot.

    The Sgt. nodded to the doctor then immediately stepped back outside – forcing the doctor to follow him. The doctor brought his mug of coffee out with him. The two men meandered to the far side of the turning-place where a Volvo hatchback with L plates on it was parked and locked up. The Sgt. spoke without looking at the doctor, grinning into the brilliant fog that had become drilled with morning sunlight from above. 'We found a dozen bottles of whisky down by the gates. The workers on the estate leave them there every Christmas; seen them sit till New Year. He forbid the workers to come up here so they left their offerings down there. The daughter told us she argued with him on Friday night before she went out. Even though she's only got her provisional she was demanding to take the car. He wouldn't let her. Course the poor bugger had drunk the house dry by then so he was pleading for her to fetch him one of the bottles from the bottom of the drive. She went out, couldn't find them in the snow so she just hitched it in to the port and with that skirt on I don't suppose she'd long to wait. She stayed two nights with friends.' The Sgt. raised his eyebrows. 'When she came back at three this morning, she found him. He must've set off when she didn't come back. Friday night.'

'Aye. To get in that state he's been out there two nights,' said the doctor, placing the mug on the roof of the car. 'She stood on his false teeth that he must have spat out shouting on his way down the track. Some of the bits had sunk right into her. Weird.'

'She's a hot buttered girl yon.'

'She is. Yes. The will is made out to the brother as well,' the doctor looked at the policeman.

'Aye. He's a tearaway bum if ever there was one. He's driving diggers or something down south but once we've contacted him he'll be up here. Within a month he'll be pissing all his share against the urinal down in The Back Settlement Hotel.'

The doctor nodded.

'That bad wee bitch inherited all the brains. He'd let the place go to rack and ruin but it's worth a lot. Three separate fishing cottages down by the river, mark my words,' said the Sgt. turning to face the doctor. 'Keep in with that wee tinker. The brother might go to pieces but this one; apart from having a shaved raw wee fanny, she'll be a power in these lands in ten years' time.'

The doctor nodded and there was silence for a while then he said, 'When your young constable left us, I told the girl I was going to give her a local anaesthetic and two injections. "Will they mark my arm?" she asked so I told her, no, she was thinking of inoculation, these were just little jabs. "In that case," she said and before I could stop her she whipped round, kneeled in a tight ball on the floor, her panties are down at her knees and her bare arse is high up in the air. "I want them both there Mr Doctor if you'd be so kind please," she smiles round at me. Honestly, I've seen it all but those stockings, the kind that

208 keep themselves up and her bent over there and me thinking what if old Andrew could see this already.'

The Sgt. shifted his feet on the gravel and declared, 'I think there's a good few lads between Little Australia and the port who've seen that sight come up before them more than the sunrise.'

Even though the dregs of his coffee were cold, the doctor lifted the mug and chuckled. He surveyed the mug thoughtfully. 'Then she said something remarkable, curled on the floor shameless, smiling back at me, "Do you know what Mr Doctor Man? I just hate it when something horrible-horrid happens to me not because Daddy's suffered, nosiree, when a horribleness happens to me I get furious. Furious at myself cause I've gone and let things get too close to me, too near, and I know I'm going to have to live with the consequences of what I've heard, or's been done to me, or I've smelt or in this case I've seen, I'm scarred and blemished by it and even if I do a horribleness to someone that's a bad thing for me, it's a blemish like my tooth," she clucked up her tongue and stuck out the roof plate with its single snow-white tooth, "Cause Mr Doctor With The Nice Hands I'm just too *good* to be bothered with blemishes and blips, I am just too *fine* for that and there's no ways I'm going to let this ugly shit of life and dying get to me. It brings me down and it cheapens me." Sit up a bit, I said, so the skin of her buttocks wasn't tautened, so she pushed herself up on her arms and giggled when I pinched a rump of her bum, then gave a wee grunt when I injected her. She was still turning staring at me when she said, "You can take off those plastic gloves, I'm *sure* your hands are warm." '

'And what did you say to that?' the Sgt. asked.

'I said, I know what you mean, Varie, through my own mind always comes the sputter of a stormlamp twenty-two years ago and my own father's white face where he'd lain down in Sorrowless Rigs Burn, the emptied whisky bottle in the left hand, the razor-sharp baling knife in the right with both wrists cut wide open but washed clean in the spate of freezing water that was going to pour his poisoned blood through the acres of land he could never make pay. She shut up after that. A hot buttered girl,' the doctor repeated.

'She's got an obscene tattoo,' the Sgt. suddenly said and the doctor nodded a grim confirmation. 'You can see it on her right shoulder blade when she wears a white blouse. If I didn't think I'd enjoy it so much I'd take a leather belt to her bare arse.'

The doctor chuckled and the Sgt. smiled for a first time. The Sgt. said, 'I'm sorry about your father. I knew him well and he was a great man.'

The doctor smiled and said, 'I've a teenage daughter myself.'

'I do too,' laughed the Sgt. 'And I'll say this, with all due respect to your father, old Bultitude is lucky; if I had *yonder* in there for a daughter and the storms that are brewing for her future I'd take myself up in those woods with a good length of rope and a fine bottle of malt.'

The doctor smiled as the Sgt. strode off. The Sgt. stopped and without turning spoke over his shoulder, 'Do call me though if you think you're going to administer another injection.'

W. N. HERBERT

FIRST FIT

'. . . three times he failed to improve upon his original
handwriting, and so today the script is preserved to us in
rubbings, with all the deletions and additions as they stood in
the first draft.'
  Lin Yutang discussing The Orchid Pavilion, *by Wang Hsichih*

Wiz ut Hogmanay or the day afore?
thi fair blarin i thi daurk
an me jist staunin ootside Boots,
whaur thi Overgait yuised tae meet thi Marketgait,
waatchin thi fisses waash past
'Muzik Express' an 'Home's Break Dancer'
stoundin fit tae be

         thi hertbeat o thi year,
birlin bairns lyk corpuscles roond,
sendin a silent clood
o doos

            tae spirl aboot
            thi City Square
and push me intae thi present.

Eh'm waatchin white bags waaltz in baldie trees
lyk some marriage atween
snaa an leaves, thi big polythene

foliage o cities. This is me *in situ*,
thi pinball afore thi shot,
wi Lin Yutang's *The Importance of Living*
in an Oxfam bag oan ma wrist,
waatchin thi fisses soom past
as tho ootwith time, observin thi recurrin
wershness o hur mou, again thi slicht
slant o his ee

                                            as tho these werr

the generaishuns fleein by:

that tough wee sockie wi thi stickin-plaistir
aa owre 'iz fiss, as tho someone trehd tae peel'um;
thi wee fat man wi a neb lyk a low wattage licht-bulb
an black cat herr thinnin oan 'iz pow; thon lass
wi the eyebrows o Nitocris an thi cough o Nicotina—
huv Eh no met thum aa afore, been marriet til thum,
hud thir bairns, intromittit wi them
in bleachin-fields and up thi closes o Coldside,
been uncled-an-auntied by thum, bullied
an brithered by thum, murdirt an touched, up an fur,
money an minny, da i thi daurk, sister still-
boarn i thi dawin, daein fur wan an doin anither—
huv Eh no been swirlin aroon thi swelchie o histry wi
ain and aa o thum, Pict & Pole & Pakistani,
Norman & Gael & Dutcher, Viking & Jew.
Northumbrian & Welsher, Roman leeins
and Armada droonlins, Eskimos oan floes
and Italians in vans: huv Eh no
been ilkane o thum hurryin thi nicht,
buyin burgirs & pehs & pittas & kebabs,
candyfloss & cola i thi cauld?

                Naw,
that's a wee bit lyk speirin
is that no Agnes Gardner that beat up Betty Mercer

212   in Dundee oan November 12th 1521
       an hud tae pey'ur fehv shillin?
       Or is that that Sandy Paterson wha complained
       'certane franschmen clum ower ma zaird dykis
       and tane away ma cale' in 1552?
       And that fast pair in thi matchin pig-bladder blousons,
       ur they no Alexander Clerke and Elesebeth Stevinsone,
       banished frae thi toon fur theft and
       'gryt sumptuos spending be nygcht continuandly'?
       And whit aboot hur in the flooer-print lycra frae Markies,
       aye, hur wi thi furst puffy bloom o vodka roond her
           een,
       shairly she's Marjorie Schireham, customar o Dundee
       atween 1326 and 1332?

                                              Naw, mebbe no.

       There's nae solvendiness tae Dundee's screed;
       uts anely alphabet is fisses and
       a screel o limbs across thi pehvment's sklate:
       a gashlin haund that's got thi shauky trummles,
       camshauchle, haurd tae read. Uts historicals's jist
       this street and thi fowk scrievat oan ut,
       fleerin and fleein lyk pages burnin, ink fadin.
       There's nae set text tae net a shoal o,
       lyk sparlins fae thi Tay, jist thi constantly
       beginnin rebrimmin o a leid,
       thi crop o thi waatir, usually crappit in by laddies
       or a coo, probably pollutit by a limepit,
       not potable, splore-pearls o tint voices.

       Tae even sey ye hear ut's tae mak yirsel
       MacCaliban insomniac wi stations inniz fillins
       that naebody else hiz ever tuned tae;
       tae grant yirsel an island atween yir lugs,
       a city in a whisky piggie at thi Noarth Pole.
       Tae claim ye can translate ut intae script's
       tae be thi year's new monstir, mair

cartoon than skrymmorie: a reid herrin-hog, mutatit,
mair like a history minnow, twa-heidit in
print's pollutit Swannie Ponds;
thi recoardin angle tae thi norm,
thi mornin blackie that's hauf-worm, howkin
uts ain tail oot o thi back green o Blackness,
haalin utsel back intae thi yird.

First fit – first person to be met or to enter a house on New Year's Day, considered to bring good (or bad) luck for the year; stoundin – pounding; birlin – spinning: spirlin – moving in a light, lively way; soom – swim; werchness – sourness; sockie – someone walking with an exaggeratedly masculine air; neb – nose; intromittit wi – had sex with; minny – mother; swelchie – whirlpool; leeins – leavings; speirin – asking; customar – collector of customs; solvendiness – trustworthiness; screed – a length of script; screel – squeal; sklate – slate used for writing on; gashlin – distorted, writhing; shauky trummles – nervous tremors; camshauchle – difficult to repeat; historicals – historic documents; scrievat – written; fleerin – mocking; sparlins – smelt; leid – language; crop o thi waatir – the first water taken from a well after midnight of Dec. 31st, supposed to bring good luck for the new year; splore-pearls – drops of saliva ejected by a speaker; tint – lost; whisky piggie – an earthenware container for whisky; skrymmorie – terrifying; reid hog – fish wrapped with a red ribbon, a New Year's gift; yird – earth.

HISTORY OF SOCK

Sock is sold at
M & S slave block attached
at ankle to Siamese Sibling.
Owner frees Sock
with tender snip
of plastic connective tissue.

214 Sock is an inveterate something
without a bra, or
Sock is not an invertebrate, but
Sock is no sad sack, rather
full of shapeless hopes.
Sock regards Foot
as a parasite.

Sock is navy blue with
lycra and cotton content to
easily grasp Owner's
concept of war against taste.
Sock empathises with Owner's
restraint of irrational opinion;
Sock is a logical being.

Sock does not speak to
Sibling, whether
in drawer, basket or
revolving bin of deluge.
Sibling, on the other foot, regales
Sock with unlikely tales
of their common coal and bogcotton origins.
Sibling has
creative limpings.

Sock disdains creativity, sport
and sneakers, releasing heady
pungencies as defence.
Sock disdains lawn-treading
and weeding duties:
Sock is not a piece
of garden hosiery.

Sock is lost in soiled condition,
somewhere between Saturday
laundrette and
rented flat.

Dog in Voltairean mode
pisses on Sock.

Sock regards overnight stars
as possible subspecies of the cufflink.
Sock remembers being pulled on
to Owner's hand
to be rolled over Sibling
in neat bundle. And
vice versa.

Further Dog in dog mode
sniffs and then pisses on Sock.

Owner having retraced sockless steps
locates Sock. Owner is appalled at
Sock's apparent incontinence.
Sock is reunited with Sibling
to whom Sock does not speak:
Sibling limp-ankled poet, whereas
Sock has now seen Life.

No joy

Black didn't know the difference between
Gaelic and Scots, not even when you told him,
but it was his bookshop we were reading in,
so we didn't. First his girlfriend sang some old
    keens, samey-sounding heart-stop things,
    then we gave the usual session: all-in flytings,

works outings from Hell. Now she was Irish, so
you might have thought he could be curious
what she was singing in his face, but no.

What she was saying, after, when the four
or five of us went drinking, me and Black,
Wedderburn, and some poet from Missouri,

216 was: 'You Scots have no joy. Where is the fackin
     joy?' Well I looked beneath my plate but found none.
     'Where,' she orated, ''s the joy?' chewing that fond noun.

She was getting felt up by him and drunk
quite suddenly. I thought about the Irish
girls in my family, the Torberts, who shrank
away from poverty to meet the dire
     marmalade lodges of Dundee, and got
     a nest of Protestant boys all thrown out

     of their fond fathers' miserable wills.
     I thought about them in the lip-reading mills,

their one gins at their proper Hogmanays,
their snorting snuff and swallowing small moothies,
their litanies upon each other's dying days.
I checked out Wedderburn declaiming truths
     like a Wee Free – how Burns was some humdinger—
     to a drunk girl sitting on another man's finger.

Marshalling time again for the cranial mince.

I checked my Harris tweed jacket for joy,
I checked my Donegal overcoat, since
it was a cold night for a northern boy
in the metropolis. I took my brains
     to Brasenose to check my English pockets,
     since some Scots come equipped with multi-sockets.

She told me all the way to the last tube
about joy, while I searched the white hairs on
her boyfriend's head for traces of the substance.
Perhaps the freckles on his hand would join
     up and spell it out. Surely this, if any
     hand, should be pleased, to touch both her and
          money.

Wedderburn meanwhile was far from his partner
(whose name it was) and weans, examining

the tonsils of the drab American bard for
flecks of pure joy with his fine rauchle tongue.
   'This creature,' I enquired, 'where were you going
   when you saw it last and just what was it doing?'

BY THE WATER OF LEITH I SAT DOWN AND WEPT: REFLECTIONS ON SCOTTISH IDENTITY

By Angus Calder

In an early episode of Irvine Welsh's novel *Trainspotting* the protagonist Renton is drinking on a balcony bar with his vicious 'friend' Franco Begbie, whose violent talk and gestures are annoying him. 'Rents' muses:

> Ah hate cunts like that . . . Cunts that are intae baseball-batting every fucker that's different, pakis, poofs, n what huv ye. Fuckin failures in a country ay failures. It's nae good blaming it oan the English fir colonising us. Ah don't hate the English. They're just wankers. We are colonised by wankers. We can't even pick a decent, vibrant, healthy culture to be colonised by. No. We're ruled by effete arseholes. What does that make us? . . . The most wretched, servile, miserable, pathetic trash that was ever shat intae creation.

Danny Boyle's highly successful film of the book turns this into a speech made by Rents when his fitness-minded friend Tommy, clean living so far but quite soon to die of AIDS contracted from bad needles, has led a small crew of Leith druggies up to a moorland Ben. They refuse to climb it. The reason for this transposition seems to be that the film's audiences south of Scotland will associate the country with Beautiful Highland Scenery. Removed from the complex pattern of interactions in Edinburgh where Welsh's book placed them, the words – originally thoughts prompted by the behaviour of one nasty Scot – stand out starkly (but still wittily) as a rant aimed at

Scottish identity in general. Americans and Germans will be challenged to set their romantic conceptions of Scotland against the frustrating reality of modern urban life.

For alert Scottish filmgoers the message could be more complex. At the very moment when enhanced and inflamed pride in Scotland is sustained for many of us by the successes of writers such as Welsh and film-makers like Boyle, these same creative people sound a warning: don't imagine that all the literary prizes, all the acclaim for James Macmillan's compositions, all the successes of painters like Bellany and Currie, mitigate the misery which makes drugs attractive to young people. Along with *Trainspotting*, the most publicised recent work of Scottish fiction has been James Kelman's Booker-winning novel *How Late It Was, How Late*. Kelman's protagonist is much older than Renton, much less educated and articulate, from a working-class Glasgow where drink and gambling rather than drugs are the opiates of the underdog. But the two books have this in common: to survive at all their protagonists have to get clear away from Scotland.

I recently by chance came across a paperback, *Famous Scots*, published in 1988 by an obscure London house. Its author, Ian Fellowes Gordon, concentrates on Scots who left their homeland to make their mark in England or overseas. Whimsically, he suggests that it might be best for the world in general and Scotland in particular if the whole population followed their example. '. . . If Baird and Carnegie and Reith and Adam and Mary Garden had to get out to perform their wonders, think what five million might do, sweeping across the globe. The mind boggles.' Mine does, indeed. I remember a journey across the old East Germany maybe fifteen years ago. The landscape between Leipzig and Dresden resembled much of Central Belt Scotland – an early centre of Industrial Revolution, now in decay. But in that queer place, the DDR, unemployment officially didn't exist. Everyone wore decent if unexciting clothes. At Dresden station a shabby creature shambled in front of me. Unbelievably, it was a rednosed hairy Scot, asking for the price of a cup of – whatever.

220   Recently, in Glasgow, I unwisely accepted the hospitality of a pleasant-enough-seeming stranger I met in a bar. He harangued me for hours, in his houseproud high-rise flat, on his sorrows and my inadequacies. It particularly incensed him that I sat drinking his water while he slowly consumed lager. He told me about his broken relationships with women, the court charges he was facing. When I tried to slip away, he halted me and threatened to pitch me out of his window – he was, he pointed out, a former prison officer and had been trained to batter people properly. So I submitted to his monologue. However one justifies the literary replication of the usages 'fuck' and 'fuckin' once or twice in almost every sentence, characteristic of certain circles in Edinburgh as well as in Glasgow, on this occasion they seemed to issue from the jaws of Hell. My acquaintance was inviting me to share Hell with him. And I couldn't firmly say I wouldn't join him.

Scotland has very beautiful countryside easily accessible from all major centres of population. (How claustrophobic London seems to a Scot.) It has produced gallant soldiers, great philosophers, devoted missionaries, inspired inventors, scientists and engineers, even a few politicians of integrity. It is also the land of the maudlin drunk and the dangerous drunk, of the wife-batterer in the desolate housing scheme. The words 'keelie' (lower-class person) and 'schemie' (inhabitant of a scheme) have no equivalents south of the border. The diminutive 'ie' as always projects a kind of acceptance, if not affection. It also, to state the obvious, expresses diminution. The Scot who is better off than the keelie or schemie, if only by fractions, may acknowledge and yet spurn, using these words, her or his own kind. We are bound together by a common fate which is not, much of the time, at all attractive. It is limited and limiting. Talented Scots, and even untalented ones, can earn much more money in other countries. However much we love and want our country, it doesn't seem to want most of us. Even cool, cool A.L. Kennedy, in her brilliant novel *So I Am Glad*, has

a far from underprivileged narrator, alienated in today's trendy
Glasgow, 'find herself', if anywhere, in Paris.

2

Scottish 'identity' is, of course, a myth. It is given substance
only in the corporealities of persons who imagine that they have
it. There is nothing outside consciousness which is 'identity',
though Scots may invest their individual identities in Scottish
landscape or Scottish football, Scottish poetry and music or
Scottish beef cattle.

One can demonstrate that over historic time, the prevalent
sense, or contending senses, of Scottish identity have changed.
After the Reformation, Lowland Scots who had embraced
Calvinism came to see theirs, along with ancient Israel, as
one of the 'two sworn nations of the Lord'. Other Scots,
Lowland and Highland, identified, in the long run more and
more imprudently, with the fortunes and fate of the Stewart
dynasty. The Union of 1707 and the Industrial Revolution
reduced such identities to sentiment. From the new commercial
and industrial Scotland emerged the cult of the Self-Helping
Scot, momentously exemplified by Burns and Carlyle, David
Livingstone and Andrew Carnegie. The 'man of independent
mind', born in a tiny, crowded shepherd's cottage or weaver's
flat, educated in a simple village school, or, after toilsome hours of
manual labour, by himself, attained by his own dedicated efforts
fame if not fortune. Or the mythical 'lad o' pairts', inspired by
a devoted dominie, made his way to the University, where
he subsisted on porridge and prizes, ultimately emerging as a
great divine or scholar or scientist. For family reasons which
will emerge later, I cannot help subscribing emotionally to the
Self-Help myth.

As industrial Scotland emerged, blackened with soot from
the land's own coal, the success which made Glasgow the
shipbuilding and heavy engineering centre of the Greatest
Empire the World Had Ever Seen sustained artisans and even

222 labourers as well as the great captains of industry. It is certain that very few Scots in the first decade of the twentieth century would have thought of themselves as 'colonised' by the English. We were, rather, proud coadjutors with them, not always hiding from them our sense that we were their superiors. In a *Punch* cartoon of the period, a businessman just back from London greets his aged father, who asks him how the English are getting on. 'I don't know', comes the answer. 'I only spoke to the top men.'

The bitterness which came with industrial collapse after the 1914–18 war coincided with strong interest, for a time, among Scottish Labour MPs in the idea of Home Rule and with the arrival of the Scottish National Party. Certain factors conspired to create the notion that Scots were a 'colonised' people who should 'liberate' themselves. One was the success of Irish Nationalism, sparked by an Easter Rising which was led by working-class, Edinburgh-born James Connolly. Another was the sudden creation, at Versailles, of a small host of new nation states carved from the Austrian and Russian Empires. If Latvia could be independent, why not Scotland?

Yet the only 'colonialism' affecting Scotland had been directed against Gaels by Lowlanders, with features comparable to those seen in, say, Africa – dispossession of land, erection of new towns as centres of commercial exploitation, attempts to stamp out the native language. In so far as Lowlanders were English-speakers and Englishmen joined in the Lowland effort, one might just speak without absurdity of English 'colonisation' of the Gaeltacht. However, throughout the Empire, where Highlanders of all classes proved to be as murderous and rapacious as soldiers and agents of British imperialism as any other sort of people from the UK, many Scottish Gaels prospered exceedingly. What Welsh's Renton, like a very high proportion of young Scots, chooses to forget, or perhaps never knew, is that Scots, whatever harm they did each other at home, were signally fortunate to be able to sally forth together and plunder vast territories secured by an imperial navy which employed ships built on the Clyde. Analogies with Latvia, Finland or Slovenia don't bear examination. The upsurge of Scottish Nationalism to electoral credibility in the 1960s was in part a local variant on a world wide theme, as colony after colony gained independence and Basques and Bretons and Sards began to be noisy. It also had something to do with the fact that loss of Britain's Empire meant declining job prospects in warmer places for able young Scots, now compelled to look about them at home.

The 'Kailyard' cult, which had arisen in the late nineteenth century as a complement to, rather than rival of, the triumphalist myth of Industrial Scotland, proved far too strong for the scorn of such major writers as George Douglas Brown and Lewis Grassic Gibbon. Exalting images of rural and small-town Scotland, it survived in the pages of the DC Thomson Press and was sustained by *Dr Finlay's Casebook* in the brave new world of mass TV. Clydesidism revived, too, as Scottish heavy industry came back to life with the Second World War and the post-war boom. But as bases of Scottish 'identity' both now seem almost as tenuous as, say, nineteenth-century 'Jacobitism', which was a cult for quaint Tories. The shipyards, the mines, the steelworks, have gone. 'Working men' can hardly find a basis for identity in prideful skilled work when such work is no longer there for them. Scottish agribusiness is hardly distinctive. For local councillors and intellectuals, Culture has now become the surviving option. Fortunately, Scottish art and literature and music have achieved notable feats in the last quarter of a century. While in Glasgow Culture officially replaces shipbuilding as the city's defining activity, the Scottish intelligentsia can find their Scotland and their own identity in their own activities and in the conceptions of Scotland which they themselves use and create. I rejoice that so many fine things have come out of our latest Renaissance, but feel increasingly uneasy. I am not a postmodernist; I am still enough of an old-time Marxist to look for a base as well as a superstructure. A Parliament Of Our Own Again won't provide a base unless it promotes activities and conditions of life in Scotland which widely differ from those seen south

224   of the border and elsewhere. Perhaps the most encouraging development at present is the new respect officially given to the ways in which we actually speak, and have spoken.

3

In February 1996, a truly startling anthology appeared under the aegis of the Scottish Consultative Council on the Curriculum, a body advising the Scottish Office, that mighty arm of the UKanian state which grasps out from premises close to the usually deserted building – the old Royal High School at the foot of Calton Hill, Edinburgh – earmarked as the place of the new Scottish Assembly before the attempt at devolution by the Callaghan government foundered in the referendum debacle of 1979. And lo, the new book was launched, with song and recital by real-life schoolchildren, there, in the very chamber where the new Parliament, when we get it, will probably meet. *The Kist/A'Chiste* anthology aggregates material selected and supplied by every education authority in Scotland. Some if it is written by schoolchildren themselves. Most of the individual items could be described as poetry, but there are also short stories and plays. And very little of the book is in standard English.

'Everyone knows' that after that vile Education Act of 1871 which, in the interests of the bourgeois state, made schooling compulsory, children were beaten for using at school dialects of Scots – let alone the Gaelic which regimes since the days of James VI had intermittently toyed with extirpating. Now, in complete reversal, anything goes. From the Dundee authority, one guesses, comes a comic strip of 'The Broons', that pawky family featured since what seems like time immemorial in the pages of the DC Thomson Press *Sunday Post*. Paw Broon, the diminutive cloth-capped patriarch, says to his daughter's new English boyfriend, 'I don't suppose you've ever seen a haggis? My, it's a rare bird an' awfy hard to catch – it can blaw itsel' up an' doon just like a balloon.' He invites young Cyril to join him on a haggis shoot and believes he has pulled his leg successfully as

the young Sassenach blasts away at fictitious haggises flying past.
But Cyril claims in turn that if you dig up a rabbit's burrow at
midnight you'll find a haggis sleeping there, and successfully
performs the trick. He's been working as a butcher himself,
and produces one of his own making . . .

It must have been Shetland which supplied a parody
of Masefield's 'Cargoes' in Norroena/Scots, the tongue of
those islands:

Sixareen fae Feddaland
Back ower fae North Roe
Rowin hom troo Yell Sound
In a six knot tide . . .

One infers that it was Strathclyde which sent in the much-loved
'Lament for lost dinner ticket' by Margaret Hamilton:

See ma mammy
See ma dinner ticket
  A pititnma
Pokit an she pititny
  Washnmachine . . .

There are items which could have been found in staider
anthologies – for instance, 'The Ballad of Sir Patrick Spens',
MacDiarmid's great lyric 'Empty Vessel', Derick Thomson's
Gaelic poem about the Norsemen arriving and settling on his
own island of Lewis. This last, of course, is given, like all the
Gaelic contributions, with translation in standard English facing.
But a full inventory of the contents of this extraordinary volume
would reveal, as a common distinguishing feature from Standard,
the tendency of all tongues spoken demotically in Scotland to
drive towards humour – dry, grim, warm or biting. Two
wonderful facts impress me about *The Kist/A'Chiste*. (They
might not seem so amazing to the teachers of English who

226 have for decades now been waging in schools up and down the land their guerrilla campaigns on behalf of the vernacular.) First, education authorities are now positively encouraging children to use in class the tongues they actually speak at home and in the streets. Yet, second, all these tongues are, as it were, talking to each other. Joy Hendry, editor of *Chapman* magazine, who was a prime mover for this anthology, was formerly a teacher herself, and she tells me that she used Hamilton's 'Dinner Ticket' poem with its Glaswegian phonetics in classrooms in East Lothian. Teachers in Ayrshire are now encouraged to explore Sheena Blackhall's Aberdeenshire Doric. And the book invites teachers and pupils alike to be curious about Gaelic. The book thus stands for diversity within unity.

The Scots Language Society will probably hate this. Its members seem to be hunting the snark of a single Scots language, with its own teachable grammar and national uniformity. Neil R. MacCallum, editor of the Society's magazine *Lallans*, recently wrote in his regular arts column in the SNP's *Scots Independent*, that: 'The remarkably consistent literary Scots as represented by Allan Ramsay and Robert Fergusson in the eighteenth century, through to Soutar and his younger contemporaries is a fairly standard language based on a natural spoken tongue.' It is significant that he didn't mention Burns, whose use of Scots was anything but consistent. MacCallum went on to upbraid the published text of Joy Hendry's play about Soutar for 'inconsistencies', such as using both 'school and 'skule', 'ken' and 'know'. He missed the simple point that people around Soutar would have switched tongues, as Scots generally do. A play about modern Scots couldn't have characters sticking to Language Society-approved forms and remain veridical.

I was talking about tongue-switching the other day to Paul Fernie, who comes from Leith (and is therefore an authority when he approves of the 'inconsistent' language of Irvine Welsh's fiction.) Leith-speak between Leithers is such that outsiders are barred. Paul, who works with the folklorist Hamish Henderson, has a fine story to illustrate this. Hamish invites him to meet a certain Italian in an Irish bar in Rome called the Fiddler's Elbow. The Italian's (standard) English is good and he and Paul speak easily together for some time. Then a woman friend of Paul's, also from Leith, joins them, and she and Paul begin to exchange news. The Italian is stricken with total bafflement, and tells Hamish, 'I can't understand what they're saying.' To which the great expert on Scottish song and story replies, 'Neither can I.'

The notion of a Standard Scots is exploded neatly, and I think decisively, by a squib of Tom Leonard's in his book *Intimate Voices*:

MAKARS' SOCIETY
GRAN' MEETIN'
THE NICHT
TAE DECIDE THE
SPELLIN'
O' THIS POSTER

And MacCallum, who writes with some style himself in English, should recognise that English is also a Scottish tongue. The much-loved poet Norman MacCaig, whose death just after the outburst by MacCallum which I've quoted seemed to unite all of literary Scotland as one mourning family, wrote exclusively in English, though one heard behind the voice of his poems, its quirks and its rhythms, those of Gaelic ancestors and Scots-speaking friends. Would any 'Scot' of taste care to cast out of some putative canon the splendid English prose of Hume and Stevenson? That hero of the Nationalists, Fletcher of Saltoun, who opposed the 1707 Union so eloquently, wrote smooth English of 'Addisonian' standard well before most Englishmen could.

4

On the matter of English in Scotland I am personally sensitive. I was once sitting with Hamish Henderson in his second (perhaps

228   first) home, Sandy Bell's Bar, when some sardonic youth accused me of being English because my voice is consistently rp. Hamish said, in that unmistakeable high drawl of his in which I detect, beside his native Perthshire, traces of education at Dulwich College and Cambridge University, 'Oh, no, Angus has a very *good* Scottish accent.' And of course a lot of Scots, not just Tories, use rp. In Edinburgh, rp can arouse resentment, because some folk resent the city's many English incomers, and because class divides have separated posh New Town lawyers and professors from Leith dockers and Craigmillar 'keelies'. In Glasgow I have no problem this way. People just assume that I come from Edinburgh . . .

Ironically, my mother, who did her best to make her five children speak pure rp, is from Glasgow, where she trained as an elocution teacher. Now, how can I describe my own 'Scottish identity?'

The historian Christopher Harvie once distinguished between 'Black Scots' and 'Red Scots'. The former stayed at home and, so to speak, cultivated the kail in the kailyard and stirred the porridge. The latter, Scotsmen on the make, roamed to every corner of the world.

My father was a typical Red Scot. So were his two brothers, who rose high in the aviation industry, one in England, the other in Canada. Sister Bella stayed in their native Forfar, where their father worked in a jute mill and their mother took in washing. She married a baker, and through their taking over all the town's bakeries became eventually sole owner of that remarkable comestible, the Forfar Bridie (a robust chieftain of the race of bridies, which are mostly fissenless, cheapskate things). She was a Black Scot, and an exceptionally dour one.

Dad was brilliant, but declined the chance of university and left school at 16 to become a newspaper reporter. The DC Thomson Press welcomed him. He wrote crime reports for the *Sunday Post* from Glasgow, where he met my mother, a doctor's daughter. By the time they were 21, they were married and settling in London, where Dad rose rapidly in Fleet Street. His remarkable career

later included fearless, outspoken reporting of the London Blitz, 229
hijacking by Churchill's government to head 'white' propaganda
in the famous Bletchley ensemble, great distinction as a science
writer, and a Labour Life Peerage. In the late fifties Edinburgh
University made him Professor of International Relations (and
found they had to give him an honorary MA to legitimate him,
since he had never attended any university). This eventually
occasioned a return to Scottish base at last, around the time I
was leaving university myself.

Meanwhile I had grown up in Sutton, a leafy but boring
outer suburb of London. My mother's 'Kelvinside' accent, my
father's well-tamed Forfar, were still very apparent over the
phone, and in certain tricks of speech. I did, and did not, pass
for white. Angus, after all, is a distinctively Scottish name. As a
very small boy I wore a kilt – too expensive to replace when I
outgrew it. I knew from a very early age that I was different.

My non-related 'aunties' and 'uncles', my parents' oldest
friends, were Scottish. (Scottish journalists, James Cameron and
Tom Baistow, were the only non-family people present when
they celebrated their golden wedding, along with Cameron's
Indian wife.) We did not go in for Burns Nights at home, but
on at least one Hogmanay, since our English neighbours did not
understand the custom of 'first footing', I was sent out with the
traditional shortbread, coal and salt in hand, to be readmitted
seconds later. Reels were danced in the living room, where
most of the poetry books in the bookcase were Scottish, and
in Scots.

We were Socialists living in a solidly Tory area, and
Congregationalists domiciled opposite an Anglican church.
(Our own minister, a learned and passionate preacher, was Welsh,
and a fellow-Socialist.) I attribute a lot of my many problems at
successive schools to a complex sense of difference from others.
Torment reached a peak with the Scottish gym teacher at my
grammar school. This fierce little man also instructed my mother
in country dancing at the local Caledonian Society. He taught
other boys this form of exercise, but I rejected it. I would not

230 perform his fake sword dance, either. 'The back the side, the front the back, the back the side, the front the back, CALDER STOP SCRATCHING YOUR BALLS!!!!.' It wasn't till I was thirty-five that, dragged into summer-school discos, I discovered I could dance in any way at all.

Naturally, however, my first girlfriend was the daughter of Scottish parents. And my first wife, met at Cambridge and married in England, also. I'll try to distinguish what I felt in childhood and youth, or realise now, was 'Scottish' from the Englishness around me.

A degree of warmth? I think so, though of course one knew warm English people. I imagine I'd have found this even in my ferocious gym teacher if I'd met him as an adult. Scottish combativeness in debate and abrasiveness in conversation are not incompatible with warmth. There is an innate propensity, it seems, to 'flyte', as our medieval poets did, exchanging mock abuse in competition. I have often heard men in Scottish pubs, professional men as well as working men, trading insults with great enjoyment.

Puritanism? Certainly, in Scottish circles I remember, sex was not mentioned except when some item in the news aroused cryptic disapproval. But here in Scotland itself one is aware of wide divergencies. The Burns Supper tradition offers even respectable persons disgustingly large scope for coarseness. Scottish pantomime comedy is innocently broad. Since the days of Dunbar and Lindsay, there has been tension in Scottish literature between licentiousness and restraint. The language of Covenanting propagandists positively gloats over the iniquities of those who follow the 'whore of Babylon'. Burns picked up and carried to great heights an acceptance of carnality found in popular song. Yet Burns had a puritan streak, too, seen in 'The Cotter's Saturday Night'.

Respect for intellect and science? My father embodied that, and I can barely see past him to judge others. To say that the general attitude towards education in Scotland is more favourable than elsewhere is not to endorse the dubious boast that our institutions are much superior. Yet the fact that the boast is made, and believed south of the border, so often, is in itself significant.

A democratical, 'man's a man for a' that' spirit? Well, my father talked of Elizabeth Bowes Lyon, from Glamis near Forfar, as a kind of childhood neighbour. Her common touch as George VI's consort probably saved the British monarchy in the crisis following the pro-Nazi Edward VIII's abdication. My mother's father, the only grandparent I knew, who came to spend his last days in our house, had been an early and passionate advocate of a National Health Service, had chaired meetings for Jimmy Maxton, and had treated poor patients in Bridgeton free. Though I cannot say that I encountered any Scot in my boyhood who was more radical than the Welsh Congregationalist minister whom I mentioned above, there was a general 'come on in, will ye have a dram?' spirit amongst Scots I knew; see under 'warmth' above . . . This brings me, somewhat crabwise, to two remarkable films which have recently carried images of Scotland into packed cinemas. *Braveheart* first, then *Trainspotting*.

5

I'd been very squeamish about going to see Mel Gibson's film about 'the' Wallace. When it arrived in Scotland in the autumn of 1995, attended by its swoon-making star-cum-director, the SNP had taken it up for propaganda purposes. Reports from people I respected suggested that the film was not only at an antipodes from factual history (I could stand that – Michael Caton-Jones's *Rob Roy*, which travesties early-eighteenth-century Scotland, is actually a very good Wild-South-West-Highland-Western) but also crassly and racistically anti-English.

As a professed 'cultural historian', I had to endure this film. But who to go with? Embarrassing to view it with an English friend, of whom, in Edinburgh, I have many. But my Scottish friends tend to be more-or-less nationalistic, and I dreaded some sterile wrangle afterwards. As the film neared the end of its Edinburgh

232   run, I was talking one Friday night to Joy Hendry and Joyce Macmillan, the sage and principled theatre critic and political columnist of *Scotland on Sunday*. Joy's pro-SNP but declares fiercely 'I'm *not* a patriot, Scotland's a rotten country'. Joyce is so anti-people-who-are-anti-English that she must be in line for death threats from the mercifully few nutters on the SNP's quasi-Fascist fringe. Giggling like schoolkids, we decided to brave *Braveheart* together the following Monday. But on the day, we all found alternative engagements.

In the end I appealed to my daughter Gowan; as an actor, her main interest was in watching Scottish performers in the film do their bit-parts. Brought up in Scotland, entirely State-schooled, she retains the Anglicised rp accent of both her parents (and complains that it may cost her jobs, as producers look for folk who were reared, or sound as if reared, in Glasgow or Dundee schemes, to cast for yet another despairing or sentimental touring play about slices of working-class Scottish life).

So Gowan and I sat gobbling chocolate mints through the three hours (plus compassionate intermission) of *Braveheart* in the Dominion, Morningside, where most successful movies go to die. The auditorium was barely a third full. That day the tabloid *Daily Record* had reported that the 'Braveheart effect' on the Scottish opinion polls had ebbed away. Because of the film's arrival (so legend will have it, and gullible historians will write it), the SNP had shot up to 30%. Now they were back to a 'normal' 23%.

It wasn't too bad. It was *not too* bad, really. Honestly, I mean, it wasn't *so* bad. As Gowan confessed, it was *inspiring*, actually.

There was this Aussie, Gibson, as Wallace, with a consistent and even convincing West of Scotland accent. (Better than Neeson, the Irishman who played Rob Roy in Caton-Jones's film.) Naebody kens whit the fuck The Wallace talked like. His name suggests Welsh genes. He might have got his tongue round funny-spelt words like you find in medieval Scots – 'quhilk' for 'which' and so on. He might have called women 'queans' – in Aiberdeen they are still 'quines'. He most likely knew a bit of Gaelic – most Scots seem to have had at least a trading knowledge of the Highland tongue in those days, and the poet William Neill was claiming a few years back that he still heard shepherds using it high in the Galloway hills . . . Anyway, Mel had settled for modern Strathclyde, and had a nice gallus wee grin to go with it. See you ootside, Jimmy, was his attitude to the fuckin English. He cut the throat of the English nobleman who'd cut his wife's throat, rode into the bedroom of a Scottish noble who'd deserted at the Battle of Falkirk, disposed of him, then jumped his horse oot the windae, descending hundreds of feet into the loch below. The hardest of hard men, but charming with it. Kent French and Latin, tae, a bit like one of James Kelman's fuck-saying proletarian philosophers . . .

In fact Mel, or his scriptwriter, implausibly named 'Randall Wallace', had got eerily close to the throbbing heart of our current ethnic consciousness. Oz nationalism must be the key to it. The Aussies who, as Churchill complained bitterly when they started narking at him during the Second World War, are largely descended from 'bad' Irish 'stock', tend to define themselves, basically, as anti-Pom. The Poms are all bastards and (in a non-sexual sense) poofters. (Cf. Irvine Welsh's 'wankers.') Sure enough, in *Braveheart*, those Poms who aren't extremely nasty officer types, or mindless automaton infantry, are raging queens. There are only these three types of Pom.

The first and second types, as Gibson intuits, now play rugby for England. They are big and strong and utterly convinced that they are going to beat Scotland. Usually, it has to be admitted, they do. But every so often, by guile and wit, we beat them. (What, *me* cheating ref?) Aitken and Sole, cheered on alike by latterday Miss Brodies shopping in Jenners and lager-drinking Hibees (Hibernian FC supporters) in pubs on the soon-to-be-named Irvine Welsh Heritage Trail in Leith, led canny, brave fifteens who fucked the English in two recent Grand Slams. We were smaller, see, but we were clever.

At a pregnant moment in *Braveheart*, Brian Cox, playing the boy Wallace's guardian after the English have hacked his father

234 and brother to death, says he'll teach him to read Latin before he teaches him to fight. Tapping of noddles goes on, here and elsewhere in the movie, to indicate that it's in yer heid ye beat the fuckers, ken? Sure enough, at Stirling, the Scots, relaxed among themselves, jeering warmly at each other and throwing the odd friendly punch, go in for clever tactics which fuck the English ooti sight. This is eftir they've all raised their kilts and waved their goolies in defiance.

You can do that if you're wearing a kilt. It is easy to tell who the Scots are in the movie. They wear kilts. I suppose that back in the thirteenth century, Wallace and other Lowlanders did wear plaids, and they might have belted these, producing a kilt effect. But with weather as bad as the film suggests (probably because it was shot in Ireland) they'd no hae been canny not to wear leggings as well. Gibson, though, with swaddled legs and shaggy bootees, wouldn't have had quite that shinny appeal which persuades the French lassie who'll be the next Queen of England (some quean to be a Queen, eh?) that she must sacrifice her body to him. (Without any attendants, she awaits him in a Highland bothy to warn him of her evil father-in-law's latest treacherous plan. Nae tabloid ratpack in those days – Princess Di, eat your heart out.) If the film is to be believed, monarchs enthroned in Westminster Abbey ever since descend from the loins of the Wallace – which, come to think of it, renders appropriate the role of that Abbey's choir who, along with the London (sic) Symphony Orchestra, garnish the film's soundtrack.

Scots are cheery. Scots make jokes. Kilted Scots are sexy. But Scottish toffs betray prole Scots. That's what the film says. The Bruce, an aristocrat, is a fraught character, torn between toff self-interest and prole destiny, as his large and agonised eyes display. Gowan said afterwards, with her usual acuteness, that the film was really more about class than nationality. The Scottish nobility are shown as a shifty lot, obsessed with their estates in England, and easily bribed. At one point The Wallace declares to The Bruce, 'You think this country exists to provide you with position. I think your position exists to provide our

people with freedom.' In response, The Bruce muses, 'From
top to bottom this country has no sense of itself.'

We can relate all this to mindsets characteristic of the present-day Scottish intelligentsia ... To be Scots is to be prole. To be prole is to be Socialist (so fuck off, Tony Blair, vampire from that Hammer Horror castle on a hill, Fettes College). To be Socialist is to be internationalist. So, we go so far with our Scottish nationalism, join the clamour for a Scottish Parliament, mingle as Artists for Independence, then think: hell, we're Socialists, really, internationalists really. An independent Scotland run by New Town lawyers and money men, or dominated by fixit Labour councillors from Strathclyde might even be worse than what we have now, a wee country hundreds of miles from London where people can at least unite in girning against Westminster rule. If we couldn't blame the English for most things, we'd blame each other.

Serendipitously, I'd been warmed up for *Braveheart* by a seminar that afternoon at Edinburgh University's Centre of African Studies. It was on the Oromo.

Who? Despite over thirty years of interest in African matters, despite having lived awhile in Kenya, where there are 200,000 Oromo in three groups towards the northern and north-eastern borders, I'd never heard of these people. Over half the population of Ethiopia are Oromo, yet one can read books on the country and never notice them. With European encouragement, Abyssinian kings, Amhara, overran the Oromo country, southern Ethiopia, or 'Region 4' as it is now. As discussion proceeded after a learned paper, as a couple of Oromo actually present made their rather shy voices heard, one point seemed clearer and clearer: the 20-million-plus Oromo, silenced and overruled, retain a strong sense of common identity despite sharp differences in religion and politics among themselves. Language binds them, and also a common myth of origin – all Oromo groups, inside and outside Ethiopia, trace themselves back to the same place. Kinship and intermarriage help hold identity together. But above all, if you're Oromo,

236   you're not Abyssinian. You're not Amharic. You're not Tigrean.

Scots share no one distinctive language with fellow Scots. We don't have a common myth of origin, unless it's expressed in the every-schoolboy-knows joke that the eponymous Scots originally came from Ireland. Picts, Strathclyde Britons and, yes, Angles, eventually came under the King, not 'of Scotland' but 'of Scots'. Sane Scots know that we were always mongrels. And we are exogamous with it. A typical present-day Scot will have one Highland granny and one English one, with two Lowland grandads and a lot of Canadian cousins. His Dad will have converted to Catholicism on marrying an Italian- or Polish-Scot. My daughter Gowan's origins go back, through her Scots-Jewish grandfather, to the noted ghetto of Vilnius, in Lithuania, and beyond that to the ancient Mediterranean and Middle East.

So we are not much like the Oromo except in one respect. We define ourselves by what we are *not*. We are *not* English. I talked a few months back to a bitter man in a pub who'd been made redundant by our local armament makers, Ferranti. In the package of chips on his shoulder, anti-English sentiments jutted out. You go to London. The barman sneers at you because you're a Jock. Fucking English . . . I forbore to point out that in my experience barmen in London are commonly Irish or Aussie or, yes, Scottish . . . Renton's exodus to London (then further) in *Trainspotting* echoes that of so many dissatisfied Scots.

6

In the ScotRail free magazine, which on February 1996 caught up with the boom in Scottish fiction (meaning critical and commercial success in London) A.L. Kennedy admitted to having something in common with James Kelman and Irvine Welsh. 'We have a dark sense of humour, are politically left-of-centre and not afraid of nastiness in our writing.' These characteristics link all three with Janice Galloway, Duncan McLean, Alan

Warner and the longstandingly successful Alasdair Gray and
Iain Banks. The Scotland of recent fiction has been a grim
and dangerous place. Irvine Welsh might seem extremist read
in isolation – alongside the others he appears pretty typical.
There is a latent contradiction between the left-wingness and
the nastiness. If there is any hope, such writers might say,
echoing *1984*, it lies with the proles. But the proles, rather
than banding together in search of political solutions, are barely
coping with confused suffering, and prone to self-mutilation
and self-destruction.

Were it not for the scene which I referred to at the start of
this piece, the film of *Trainspotting* might be decoded without
reference to Scotland or to politics. Young people, variously
charming and sinister, damage themselves with drugs and booze,
and get involved in petty, then major, crime in a grubby urban
setting . . . With its assured style and brilliantly judged pace,
the movie might be taken to be a local response to Quentin
Tarantino. It is a very filmy film and its musical soundtrack,
which has no obvious Scottish reference, places it firmly in the
hands of people who know about the recent past of rock. (The
setting, carefully sustained, is the mid-Eighties.)

The specificity of Welsh's Leith and Edinburgh is lost, despite
shots of Princes Street and the Castle. Not only is dense Leith
idiom avoided, but the accents suggest West as much as East,
in Lowland Scottish terms, and local eyes spot the signs that the
outside shooting was mostly done in Glasgow. But Renton's
outburst about English wankers and shitty Scots ensures that
the film is a statement about Scotland, as well as applicable to
all cities . . . Not only the violence of Begbie, but the mental
sickness of Sick Boy and the gormless, compulsive thieving of
Spud are seen as examples of enslaved and colonised Scottish
mentality. When these three confront a suave English drug
baron to sell him the heroin which they have stolen, Renton,
psychologically bystander rather than participant, reflects that
such a big operator is bound to make suckers of them – and
he does. As the only significant English character in the film,

238   this creep might be taken to represent all the 'colonisers', the Southrons who manipulate and control Scotland.

Virtues attributed to the Scots are set in ironic light. The braininess of Sick Boy is misapplied to endless drivel about Sean Connery movies. Social sodality, warmth and bonhomie are travestied in a scene where a baby dies and drug-taking mother howls as our charming heroin users sleep through their trances. *Braveheart* solidarity between Renton and his friends is merely an accident arising from a common background; at the end, Renton rejects Begbie and Sick Boy, purloins their share of the price of the drugs, and hands money back only to the good-natured, helpless Spud. Such discrimination accompanies a moral victory over his environment: his Scottish environment.

But all this negativity has positive implications, thanks to Renton's political rant, which suggests that *if only* the Scots could free themselves, then they might be absolved from the universal types of folly which he and his friends represent. Remove English rule: cure social disease? Maybe. Maybe.

Hypers of Scottish Culture should have problems with the *Trainspotting* phenomenon. The image of Scotland which book and film insist on presenting is very nasty, very unheathery. Both times I saw the film, early in its run at the Cameo, Tollcross – where artistically significant movies like *Reservoir Dogs* and *Carrington* play for weeks to full houses – looking around the packed audience I seemed to see almost nobody over 30. Irvine Welsh's sales, huge, especially in Edinburgh, mean that young people feel they must buy his books. The phenomenon is uncontrollable and could be lasting. I am glad that I enjoy Welsh's books, uneven though they are. I myself am not, I hope, swimming outside the current which is flowing to wherever it will flow, with whatever political, social and ethical consequences, over the year of millennium, into an unimaginable future Scotland where Scottish identities, surviving, as I am sure they will, are constructed in ways which I cannot foresee, through language in its habitual state of flux and new songs transforming old ones.

AUTHOR BIOGRAPHIES

Candia McWilliam

Candia McWilliam was born in Edinburgh in 1955. She has written three novels, *A Case of Knives*, *A Little Stranger* and *Debatable Land*, all published by Bloomsbury. She has three children.

Michael Cannon

I attended a secondary school until the age of 17 and left without intentions of going on to further education. I became an apprentice engineer, but left after around a year. I then worked for the Inland Revenue but was pathetically bad as a Civil Servant. I stuck that out for about a year also and then left to take up whatever desultory occupations I could to make ends meet: I worked as a labourer on a building site, a warehouseman, a general dogsbody in a factory manufacturing carpet sweepers. I painted lamp posts for a local authority. I took all the money I had out of the bank and went to America to return less than two months later with no money and no prospects. I then worked in the Shetland Islands doing elementary logistics for a company which helped contruct an oil terminal. These are just some of the jobs. There are more.

I eventually decided to return to full time education. At the age of 23 I attended a College of Further Education to study for exams to gain admittance to university. At 24 I went to Glasgow University and graduated four years later with an honours degree.

240   I currently live and work in Glasgow. I've had one novel, *The Borough*, published in 1995 and have a second, *A Conspiracy of Hope*, being published in 1996. I am currently working on a third.

Carol Ann Duffy

Carol Ann Duffy was born in Glasgow in 1955. After reading philosophy at Liverpool University, she moved to London, where she now lives. Her *Selected Poems* are published by Penguin and her poetry has received several awards in Britain and America, including The Whitbread and Forward prizes in 1993, and the Lannan Literary Award in 1995. She has one small daughter.

William Boyd

William Boyd was born in West Africa in 1952 of Scottish parents. He was educated at Gordonstoun School and Glasgow University. He is the author of two collections of short stories and six novels, which include *A Good Man in Africa*, *The New Confessions* and *The Blue Afternoon*. His seventh novel will be published in 1997.

Kate Clanchy

Kate Clanchy was born in Glasgow in 1965, and educated in Edinburgh and Oxford. She now lives in London and works as a teacher, and as a critic for *The Scotsman*. She won an Eric Gregory Award in 1994. Her work featured in *Anvil New Poets 2*, edited by Carol Ann Duffy, in 1995. Her own first collection, *Slattern*, was published by Chatto and Windus in 1996. The *Observer* said of this book, 'Kate Clanchy is a real discovery. It is possible to imagine her becoming a genuinely popular poet, not because she writes down to her audience but because she writes of what they know in such a way that we come to know it better.'

Irvine Welsh

Irvine Welsh lives in Amsterdam. His first book, *Trainspotting* (1993), has been dramatised and filmed to enormous acclaim. His collection of stories, *The Acid House* (1991) and his second novel *Maribou Stork Nightmares* (1995) will be similarly translated. His most recent work, *Ecstasy* (1996) was the first paperback original to be a number one bestseller.

Robert Crawford

Robert Crawford's collections of poetry include *A Scottish Assembly* (Chatto, 1990), *Talkies* (Chatto, 1992), and *Masculinity* (Cape, 1996). His critical books include *Devolving English Literature* (OUP, 1992) and *Identifying Poets* (Edinburgh UP, 1993). He is Professor of Modern Scottish Literature in the School of English at the University of St Andrews, and once co-authored a pantomime.

Alasdair Gray

Alasdair Gray was born in Glasgow in 1934. He lives by painting and writing and has written thirteen books since his first novel, *Lanark*, was published in 1981. In 1986 he began working on *The Anthology of Prefaces*, a book of introductions to vernacular masterpieces in English, by their authors, arranged chronologically with historical and biographical notes. It will be completed in 1998.

Don Paterson

Don Paterson was born in Dundee in 1963. *Nil Nil* (Faber) was published in 1993, and won the Forward Prize for Best First Collection. He was a recent winner of the Arvon/Observer poetry competition. He also works as a jazz guitarist, and co-leads the jazz/folk ensemble *Lammas*. His new collection, *God's Gift to Women*, will be published in early 1997. He currently divides his time between London and Scotland, more through confusion than choice.

Shena Mackay

Shena Mackay was born in Edinburgh (in 1944) and lives in London. She has written two novellas, three collections of short stories and seven novels. Her novel *Dunedin* and the story collection *The Laughing Academy* were given Scottish Arts Council Book Awards, and she has been shortlisted for the McVitie's Prize. Her latest novel, *The Orchard On Fire*, (Heinemann) was published this year.

Robin Robertson

Robin Robertson is from the north-east of Scotland but now lives and works in London. His poetry appears regularly in the *London Review of Books* and the *New Yorker*. His first collection, *A Painted Field*, will be published by Picador in February 1997.

Douglas Dunn

Douglas Dunn's most recent collection is *Dante's Drum-kit* (Faber & Faber, 1993). His most recent collection of stories is *Boyfriends and Girlfriends* (1995) and he has edited *Scotland. An Anthology* (HarperCollins), *The Faber Book of Twentieth-Century Scottish Poetry*, and *The Oxford Book of Scottish Short Stories*. He is Professor and Head of English at the University of St Andrews, and Director of the St Andrews Scottish Studies Institute.

Tom Leonard

Tom Leonard's *Reports from the Present* is published by Cape and *Intimate Voices* by Vintage.

Janice Galloway

Janice Galloway was born in Ayrshire where she worked in a variety of paid and unpaid jobs before earning her living as a writer. Her first novel, *The Trick is to Keep Breathing* (shortlisted for the Whitbread First Novel and Scottish First Book) won the MIND/Allan Lane Award and has been staged in adaptation at the Tron Theatre in Glasgow, the Du Maurier Theatre in Toronto and the Royal Court in London. Her first collection of short stories, *Blood*, was a New York Times Notable Book of the Year. For both books, she received the American Academy of Arts and Letters E M Forster Award. Her last novel, *Foreign Parts*, won the 1994 McVitie's Prize for Scottish Writer of the Year. A new collection of stories, *Where You Find It*, was published by Cape this May.

Gordon Legge

Gordon Legge has published three books: *The Shoe*, *Inbetween Talking About Football*, and *I Love Me, Who Do You Love?* (all published by Polygon). *Question Number Ten* is taken from *Near Neighbours*, a collection of stories which will probably be published by somebody at some point or other.

Iain Crichton Smith

Born 1928 in Glasgow. Brought up in the Island of Lewis. Writes in Gaelic and in English. *Selected Stories* and *Collected Poems* from Carcanet Press, Manchester.

A. L. Kennedy

A. L. Kennedy was born in Dundee in 1965. She has published two collections of short stories, *Night Geometry And The Garscadden Trains* and *Now That You're Back*, and two novels, *Looking for the Possible Dance* and *So I Am Glad*, winning awards

244 including the Saltire Award, Mail on Sunday/Llewellyn Rees Prize, Somerset Maugham Award and the Encore Award. She is listed among the Granta/Sunday Times Best of Young British Novelists. Her first full length film *Stella Does Tricks* will be released shortly. Her next book *Original Bliss* – short stories and a novella – will be published by Jonathon Cape in the Spring of 1997. She has sold brushes door-to-door with little or no success.

Edwin Morgan

Born Glasgow 1920. Books include: *Collected Poems* (Carcanet, 1990), Rostand's *Cyrano de Bergerac*, translated into Scots, (Carcanet, 1992), *Sweeping Out of the Dark* (Carcanet, 1994). *Collected Translations* due out from Carcanet in Autumn 1996. Most recent poetry is a sequence of ten poems, *Beasts of Scotland*, written for jazz setting by saxophonist Tommy Smith (Linn Records, 1996). *A Voyage* was commissioned by the BBC and broadcast on Radio 4 on 12 June 1996.

John Burnside

John Burnside was born in 1955, in Fife, Scotland. Until recently he wrote mainly poetry, publishing five collections, including *The myth of the twin*, (Jonathon Cape, 1994) and *Swimming in the flood*, (Jonathon Cape, 1995). He received the Geoffrey Faber Memorial Award in 1994; *The myth of the twin* was selected for The New Generation Poets, and shortlisted for the T. S. Eliot prize. His first novel, *The Dumb House*, will be published by Cape early in 1997, alongside a new collection of poetry, entitled, *A normal skin*. After a long absence he has returned to his native country, and now lives in Cellardyke, in Fife.

Duncan McLean

Duncan McLean has published a book of stories, *Bucket of Tongues*, and two novels, *Blackden* and *Bunker Man*. He has also written for the stage and television, and is currently working on a non-fiction book about Bob Wills and his Texas Playboys.

Kathleen Jamie

Kathleen Jamie was born in 1962. She studied Philosophy at Edinburgh University. As well as poetry, she has published a travel book about Northern Pakistan: *The Golden Peak*, (Virago 1992). Her poetry has won several awards, including a Somerset Maugham Award 1995 and The Geoffrey Faber Memorial Award 1996. She lives in Fife.

Alan Warner

Alan Warner was born in Argyll in 1964 and brought up there. He is currently living in Spain. His novel, *Morvern Callar*, was shortlisted for the Whitbread First Novel Award and is being filmed by the BBC. His second novel, *Three Demented Lands*, a sequel to *Morvern Collar*, will be published by Jonathon Cape early in 1997.

W. N. Herbert

W. N. Herbert was born in Dundee in 1961, and educated there and at Brasenose College, Oxford. His D.Phil on the poetry and prose of Hugh MacDiarmid was published by the OUP in 1992 as *To Circumjack MacDiarmid*. Since 1993 he has held writer's residencies in Dumfries and Galloway, and Morayshire. He is currently Northern Arts Literary Fellow at Newcastle and Durham Universities. He writes in both Scots and English. His books include *Sharawaggi* (with Robert Crawford), *Dundee Doldrums, Anither Music, The Testament of the Reverend Thomas Dick*, and *Forked Tongue* (Bloodaxe, 1994). Despite being no better nor worse than the rest, this last volume was a PBS Recommendation, a New Generation title, won a SAC award, and was shortlisted for the T. S. Eliot and Saltire prizes, so there you go. His latest volume of poems, *Cabaret McGonagall*, was published by Bloodaxe in May, 1996. Eccentric but visionary publishers might like to note he is currently completing a volume of short stories entitled *Virtual Scotland*.

Angus Calder

More Scots play cricket than go curling: Angus Calder does both. Author of *The People's War: Britain 1939–45* and *Revolutionary Empire*. His second Scottish Arts Council Book Award (1994) was for *Revolving Culture: Notes from the Scottish Republic*. His forthcoming books are a volume of poems from Diehard, *Walking in Waikato*, and *Time to Kill: The Soldier's Experience of War in the West 1930–1945*, co-edited with Paul Addison for Pimlico. He is joint inventor with Jay Hendry of the vegetarian haggis and sole inventor of the bacon, lettuce and lime pickle sandwich, which he eats for breakfast most days.